ROBERT HEYWOOD
OF BOLTON

ROBERT HEYWOOD

ROBERT HEYWOOD OF BOLTON

BY

W. E. BROWN, M.A.

First Published by S.R. Publishers Limited
1970

Published 1970 by S.R. Publishers Limited
East Ardsley, Wakefield, Yorkshire

ISBN 0 85409 643 4

Reproduced and Printed by
Alf Smith & Co. (Bfd.) Bradford, Yorkshire

PREFACE

Robert Heywood took great care of his letters and papers. His family have inherited this interest in records, and his daughter Mary Haslam edited printed editions of his travel diaries — the originals are in Dr. Williams's Library. Many of the papers were handed over to others to ensure their preservation, and these appear to have been irrecoverably lost. But a box of miscellaneous documents remained, and this was handed to me by his grandsons, Oliver Heywood Haslam and William Heywood Haslam, with a request that I should write the memoir of their grandfather. To piece out the imperfections of the documents I have used material available in the Bolton Reference Library and I am very grateful to the Librarian and his staff for the help they have given me. The Robert Heywood papers are to be deposited in this library after this book is published.

It may be in place here to add a word about Robert Heywood's family. He would have been proud of their public record. His eldest son John, a barrister, was one of the first nonconformists to enter Cambridge University when the religious tests were removed. He was twice Mayor of Bolton. Mary the daughter, (who married William Haslam), gave a lifetime of public service, particularly as the first woman Guardian in Bolton, and at the time of her death it had been proposed that she should be made a freeman of the borough.

I wish to thank the Manchester University Press for permission to quote a passage from *Public Order in the Age of the Chartists* by F.C. Mather.

1. THE UNITARIAN COTTON MANUFACTURER

Robert Heywood came of vintage Puritan stock. The home of his family, Little Lever, four miles from Bolton and within the parish, produced from the manor house in Tudor times two of the outstanding pioneers of Elizabethan Puritanism, John and Thomas Lever. Bolton itself was so Calvinist that it became known as 'the Geneva of the North'. One of the Heywoods of Little Lever, Oliver, educated at Bolton Grammar School, a Presbyterian clergyman ejected from his living in 1662, became one of the most important nonconformist ministers of the first generation. From his brother Nathaniel were descended the Heywoods of Manchester, very prominent as Unitarian liberals in the nineteenth century. Our Heywoods of Bolton could not trace a direct descent from these more famous Heywoods, but they were interrelated and they too were Unitarians and liberals.

Robert's grandfather lived in Little Lever and wove fustians, the local cloth made of linen warp and cotton weft, which had been the speciality of the Bolton district since 1600. He is said to have been one of the first men to acquire and use a spinning mule. The early mules, invented by Samuel Crompton of Bolton, were worked by a hand wheel and could be installed in a cottage. For the first time it was possible to spin on one machine all grades of yarn from the strongest and coarsest to the finest muslin yarn, hitherto beyond the skill of English spinners. Fustians became obsolete when cotton yarn of sufficient strength for the warp could be produced on Arkwright's water frame or Crompton's mule.

John Heywood, Robert's father, was one of a family of twelve, and as a boy earned a penny a week by reading a newspaper to a group of villagers. He moved from Little Lever to Bolton, where he became a member of the Bank Street Unitarian Chapel — the original nonconformist chapel in Bolton, built in 1697. He worked as a taker-in to Thomas Naylor, a manufacturer of fustians and later of quiltings, of Mount Pleasant, Little Bolton. Here the Heywoods lived, in Bury Street, until 1824, and here, when Thomas Naylor died in 1803, John Heywood set up his own business. Next door was the Swedenborgian chapel where Samuel Crompton played the organ, and Crompton was a friend of the family. On the other side was John Whitehead — a close friend whose son invented the torpedo. The fields were still just beyond them, and below the hill the River Croal swept round in a sharp curve, and at Church Wharf the Manchester and Bolton Canal, constructed in 1791, had its terminus. On a bold bluff beyond the river stood the Parish Church and the old Grammar School. The Croal divided Bolton into two townships and manors, Great and Little Bolton, which at the time of Robert Heywood's birth together had a population of about 10,000.

Robert Heywood was John Heywood's only son, born in 1786. His mother died soon afterwards; his father married again and had two more children, Hannah and Mary, the latter a crippled and backward child who died when she was fifteen. They were a close-knit family, and Robert had a genuine affection for his stepmother but the early death of his mother may have been a part cause of his intense and almost morbid attachment to his father.

When he was an old man Robert Heywood gave a talk at Bank Street Chapel about his early education. After spending some time at a dame's school very near home he was sent to a school in Folds Road, a large room filled with boys and girls, 'not on the silent system'; once he startled his mother by bringing home a live cock he had won as a prize on Shrove Tuesday. At the age of seven he went to Bolton Grammar School, whose headmaster at that time was the Rev. Joseph Lemprière, author of one of the best classical dictionaries of the eighteenth century. But Lemprière did not stay long in Bolton. Robert saw him beat a boy unmercifully before the whole school, and for this beating the governors dismissed him. Whether because of this or because the school was too old-fashioned, Robert's father removed him after he had been there only a year or so, and after a spell at a clergyman's school, sent him to a new Unitarian school.

It had been customary for the ministers at Bank Street to teach as well. Philip Holland in particular had kept a very good school to which the great potter Josiah Wedgwood had sent his sons as boarders. Now his nephew John Holland was the minister, and started a small coeducational school. Both Robert and his half-sister Hannah attended this school; the fees were four guineas a year. The group of Unitarian schoolfellows whom he met there remained his friends for life.

John Holland was a kindly and sensitive teacher, to judge by the school reports which Robert preserved, written on the receipts for fees. At first he was critical of Robert's inability to control his 'risible faculties' — for which he was known in school as 'Bursting Bob'. When the boy was ten Holland wrote: 'If Robert Heywood either played less or devoted some portion of his time at home to prepare him for school he would probably make greater progress in useful knowledge.' At thirteen 'this good-natured youth is very ready to serve and oblige. The study of the French language (an extra) takes up much of his time and may have retarded his progress in other branches of knowledge.... R.H. has the love of wisdom and will succeed in the pursuit by using diligence and taking time.' Again: 'My opinion remains the same as before of his character and disposition, that he may be persuaded to anything reasonable, that he cannot be compelled to what is wrong and that judicious praise and liberal encouragement will influence him more than censure and reproof.'

The kindly atmosphere of this school is best revealed by a comment of Holland's on Hannah Heywood. 'It may not be easy, though it is always right, to be patient and composed with those who appear to be slow, but when they have so many good properties as H.H. seems to have, such as attention, kindness, honesty and good behaviour they ought never to despair of themselves. Probably we are all dunces in some things and Sir Isaac Newton was thought a blockhead till he attended to Mathematics.' He praised Robert's 'kind assistance' to her. They had dancing lessons together in spite of their puritan background, and both studied music. Her father bought a harpsichord for Hannah. Robert learned to play the organ, and in later years bought one and installed it at home.

In 1803 when Thomas Naylor died Robert became his father's partner in the new concern of John Heywood and Son, quilting manufacturers, but his father held the purse strings very firmly, and even when he was in his thirties Robert had to ask his father for the money to go on holiday. The business was run from a warehouse from which the weavers collected the yarn they wove in their homes, bringing a piece of cloth every week, usually on a Monday, which the taker-in inspected and paid for. In this period Manchester was the main market for Bolton's cotton goods, and so that Robert could specialize in the selling side of the business his father sent him to Manchester for six months to learn marketing. The firm acquired a warehouse in Manchester, and for many years Robert Heywood travelled there weekly, usually on Saturday, at first by the canal boat, and in later more prosperous times by gig, to sell their cloth to merchants on the Exchange.

The firm prospered tranquilly. John Heywood was very cautious and continued to live simply. He is said to have become rich by extreme thrift rather than by the expansion of his business. He accumulated far more capital than he could use in his business, and the firm could always draw on some to stave off trouble in depressions. Most of the family wealth was invested in loans, mainly through mortgages, bringing in between 4% and 5% interest. John Heywood lent £5,100 to the Ashworths, Quaker cotton spinners from whom he bought his yarn, to help them to finance the re-equipment of the New Eagley Mills in 1824. He also made loans to the Slaters, an excessively adventurous firm of bleachers who bleached his cloth and who had several financial crises. Throwing good money after bad, Robert Heywood eventually had to foreclose on James Slater's Crescent Bleachworks on the Irwell at Salford, and when he could not get a tenant went into bleaching for himself. Another foundry venture which he financed at Atherton, run by the son of the Unitarian minister there, was a failure. Bankruptcies and foreclosures were frequent and troublesome; one foreclosure provided them with a small landed estate at Entwistle. When John Heywood died he left £36,000.

On the manufacturing side the business remained entirely conservative until the end in 1854. It was so difficult to adapt the power loom to the weaving of quiltings for fancy waistcoats — their staple product — that it was still possible in the 1850's for hand looms to compete with power looms. In marketing Robert was always far more enterprising than his stay-at-home father. A school friend Richard Marsden went to Gibraltar to exploit the continental market when the European ports under Napoleon's control were blocked by the Continental System; in 1811 and 1812 Robert Heywood was writing to him about the possibility of doing business there — they had fustians and India jeans as well as quiltings to sell. Marsden was discouraging. An expansion of business depended on Wellington winning victories in Spain, and in any case quiltings were not very easy to sell in Gibraltar. After the war Robert began to build up a connection with London merchants who sold on commission, and in the end this became the only outlet for the firm's cloth, and the Manchester warehouse was closed down in 1830.

John Heywood was in active control of the business until his health began to fail in the early 1820's. Charles Darbishire, Robert's closest friend, was brought in as a partner in 1822, eventually receiving one third of the profits. In religion and politics as well as in business the two men were closely associated. Darbishire was very active at Bank Street Chapel, and was a radical with more fluency and vehemence of speech than Heywood. He took on the main burden of managing the warehouse; one man who wove for the firm knew him well, but had never met either of the Heywoods. In fact Robert valued his leisure, took holidays freely and often, and always had time for public affairs. He attended to the selling by an occasional visit to London to combine business with pleasure. He was the moneyed partner and expected Darbishire to be much more consistent in attendance than he was himself.

Even when Charles Darbishire was heavily burdened with public duties as Mayor in 1839, Robert Heywood wrote him a very critical letter about the defects in the cloth which he had seen on one of his obviously rare visits to the warehouse, and he even threatened to withdraw from the partnership unless there was an improvement. Darbishire's reply pointed out that the magistrates' court on Mondays had interfered with his attendance at the warehouse at the time when most of the cloth was received. It is not surprising that after this there was considerable talk of breaking up the partnership, from which Darbishire retired in 1842, at the age of 45. Their friendship was unimpaired.

Two reminiscences of Robert Heywood's business life are to be found in *Historical Gleanings of Bolton and District,* by B.T. Barton. The first was a note from a Mr Traice: 'Though a liberal in politics he used to express his admiration of the Prince Regent; and as few of his friends shared this admiration, he would tell them, with a pleasant smile, that his firm manufactured fancy waistcoatings, and the Prince set the generous example of having the vest made entirely of the same material, thus using twice as much as if the back had been made of some cheap fabric..... He used to drive from Bolton to Manchester market, and he would dine at one of the ordinaries; but instead of joining the other guests as they smoked their pipes and imbibed their toddy, he strolled about among the old book shops and stalls till it was time to go on 'Change. Thus he had not only made himself acquainted with much curious literature, but he rarely came home without some books in the box under the gig seat.' The second came from a woman who had worked as a little girl at Mount Pleasant Mill in Bury Street, opposite John Heywood's house, warehouse and garden: 'Against the front wall of this house, and up to the public thoroughfare, unprotected and unmolested, was a Jargonelle pear tree, which I have seen covered with blossoms or loaded with fruit as the seasons came. Mr Robert Heywood often occupied a quiet half hour with reading whilst sitting or walking in the garden.'

John Heywood's only known journey was a visit to Lancaster on jury service; his wife spent her first night away from home 25 years after her marriage, when she visited relatives in Leeds, and Robert gave her her husband's only message, 'cum wum'. By contrast Robert Heywood became probably the most travelled man in Bolton. His appetite for new places and his interest in a wide range of pleasures, recreations and cultural activities softened the austerity of his puritanism.

Returning from a visit to London in 1810 he stayed with a friend in Retford, went fishing, and visited stately homes, Clumber Park, Worksop Manor and Chatsworth — the grandest house he had ever seen, with waterworks which 'beggared description'. From there he walked to Castleton in the Peak, saw Peak's Hole and Speedwell mine, and travelled by boat underground for 750 yards to reach a cavern. From Castleton he walked to Manchester, went to the races on Kersal Moor, and returned home by the canal packet.

Throughout his life Robert Heywood was a great walker. In an account of a visit to the Lakes in 1813 he writes of leaving Ulverston early and 'brushing off the dew' with a four mile walk before breakfast. On his third visit to Ireland in 1825 he climbed Mangerton, the nearest mountain to Killarney. 'Hired a guide for 3/- and left Killarney at nine. Ascending the mountain met a very nice clean family — took some goat's milk for which I gave 1/- and 2d. to a lad for a song. As we proceeded up the mountain met by other children with goats and milk. Came to Horse Glen, sat down and partook of some gooseberry pie and some neat whisky. Walked to the summit, threw stones down the precipice. Came to the Devil's Punch Bowl, found some more little girls with goats' milk, devoured the bread and butter and drank whisky...... Saw an eagle above the mountain.' Those were early days for mountain walking, but evidently it was already an organized activity in Killarney.

It was not until he was thirty, in 1816, that Robert Heywood first went abroad. Marsden, on his way home from Gibraltar, suggested a rendezvous in Paris. Robert had much difficulty in persuading his father to let him go. Fortunately it was haytime and as the weavers would be in the fields there would be little cloth to take in — industry in Little Bolton was still somewhat rural. Even so he could find time for only three days in Paris.

From the time of his Irish visit Robert Heywood kept a diary of each journey overseas, and four accounts (Italy 1826, America 1834, the Levant 1845, and Russia 1858) were privately printed by his daughter in 1919. In 1826, to the great trepidation of his father, he made his first extensive continental journey, to France and Italy — as far as Naples — and back to Switzerland, the Rhine valley and the Netherlands. This Grand Tour lasted three months and cost £100. His diary reveals only a very stereotyped appreciation of the art treasures of Italy, but a lively interest in people, including his fellow travellers, and in social facts, and a vivid sense of the hardships and discomforts of travelling. A coach journeying through the Appenines was drawn by six horses and four oxen, and was supplied with five postilions and a military escort. Once, when his sailing ship was becalmed in a small port on the Gulf of Genoa, from which escape was impossible by land and where he suffered badly from bugs and fleas in a primitive inn, he hired a rowboat with three rowers to make his getaway across the gulf.

Everywhere on his journeys abroad Heywood made use of introductions provided by Manchester merchant friends to their continental representatives. In Rome he was nobly entertained by the principal of the English Jesuit College, and he toured the city escorted by two student guides. He was amused at the thought of the shock it would have given his Unitarian friends in Bolton to see him escorted by two young men in cassocks. To him the climb of Mount Vesuvius was the most memorable event of his holiday. Heywood lived very simply when he was abroad; he distrusted foreign food and lived largely on a diet of eggs, boiled milk, bread, fruit and plenty of wine — a teetotaller at home, he always allowed himself intoxicating drinks when he was on holiday.

From his early manhood Robert Heywood was one of the most prominent laymen at Bank Street. He was coopted a trustee of the chapel at the age of 25, and already he taught a Sunday School class. For very many years he was superintendent of the Sunday School. The scholars were ushered into the morning service after their own meeting, and he kept a stern eye on their behaviour. For over fifty years he taught reading and writing to a young men's class, characteristically making economies by the greater use of slates and slate pencils, but his attempts to get them to attend arithmetic classes on week nights did not succeed.

He helped the chapel generously with money. In particular in 1835 he was the chief contributor to a fund to clear an obstruction to the entrance to the chapel by buying and pulling down a public house, the Old Wheatsheaf. For over forty years he was the treasurer of the chapel. He also had some wider interests in the Unitarian movement, and for much of his life he was treasurer of the Fund for Ministers' Widows.

Robert Heywood held strongly to his Unitarian beliefs. His friends were nearly all fellow members. He objected to 'mixed' marriages between Unitarians and Anglicans. He reported to John Holland a curious happening in 1816 which arose from his zeal. When he was travelling back from Manchester in the canal boat one Saturday evening, he persuaded a young man he knew, one of a party of Methodists returning from a conference, to borrow and read a Unitarian pamphlet. Heywood and a friend decided to walk along the towpath between locks, and while he was out of the boat the pamphlet was passed round the Methodist party, who made fun of it, and finally one of them threw it into the canal. When he rejoined the party on the boat and discovered what had happened there was a furious quarrel and he came very near to throwing the youth into the canal after the pamphlet.

With all the assurance that wealth gives in a church without a hierarchy, Robert

Heywood became the mouthpiece of a group of critics of John Holland's preaching. He excused his blunt words to his old schoolmaster as upholding 'the democratical rather than the monarchical system' in religion. He said that most of the congregation found the sermons 'abstruse and uninteresting', and asked for 'more moral and practical preaching'. There was a good deal of friction in this congregation, which was much given to theological and political argument, and lacked leadership in John Holland's later years as his powers failed. When he was forced by ill-health to retire in 1820 a serious split occurred. Robert Heywood and his fellow trustees proposed, and carried in the congregation by a majority of six, the appointment of Noah Jones, a young and inexperienced recruit from the Congregationalists (he later married Charles Darbishire's sister). Deep divisions came to a head and a powerful minority group, which seems to have included the strongest radicals in politics, seceded and started a new congregation in a former Baptist Chapel in Moor Lane. For a while, led by a vigorous minister, they carried all before them, and in 1823 Heywood reported a congregation of nearly 300 there, while the attendance at Bank Street was 120.

Noah Jones left Bank Street after one year, and after a long delay Franklin Baker was appointed minister in November 1823. He rebuilt the Bank Street congregation. Gradually the secessionists drifted back, and at last in 1839 the two congregations were amalgamated. Baker was a really distinguished man who contributed much to the cultural interests of Robert Heywood's circle and to the life of Bolton. For forty years he was a leader of nonconformist liberalism in the town. He was the uncle of an Archbishop of Canterbury (Benson), and his brother was knighted whilst Lord Mayor of Manchester.

Robert Heywood owed much of his rugged character to his religion. Cobden, commenting on the insatiable love of caste in England, pointed out that for many it was religion − the old nonconformity now largely Unitarian, Congregationalist and Baptist − that had prevented assimilation into the class system. Walter Bagehot described Victorian England as a 'deferential society,' but he admitted that there was less deference in Lancashire than in other parts of England. Lancashire Unitarians, conscious of their pedigree and traditions and their aloofness from the main stream of Anglican religious and social life, kowtowed to no one. Heywood had no difficulty in mixing on terms of equality with foreign aristocrats; he took it for granted that he should meet the President of the United States and the ruler of Egypt. He had an undisguised contempt for the idle and spendthrift, however aristocratic.

He lived an abstemious life. A strong believer in early rising, he read − books not periodicals − for an hour before his frugal breakfast of a boiled egg. He was a stern opponent of smoking and intemperance. He could be hard on the improvident, especially among his needy relatives, but he was usually generous to people who were doing their best under difficulties and who needed his help. He was no mere killjoy; his recreational interests ranged from discussion groups and orchestral concerts to billiards, for which he kept up an annual subscription for some years.

The breadth of Robert Heywood's cultural interests speaks well for the Unitarians of Lancashire. He was of course born into a family that was already prospering, and he always had — and insisted on having — a good deal of leisure. He was not highly educated at school, although he found the French which he learned there extremely helpful in his travels in Europe. Travel enlarged his interests, but basically he owed his culture to his circle of Bank Street friends. His journals and letters display a lively curiosity but no originality of mind, and his few remaining formal writings are dull.

Heywood built up a good library of books. He recorded many purchases in his diaries, including the entire works of Swift and Scott, and an encyclopedia in 72 volumes which he bought for £43 in 1818. The high spot of his book collecting was the buying of the Bowyer Bible in 1856. William Bowyer, one of a family of distinguished London printers, published a handsome edition of the Bible in 1800, and printed a special copy on large sheets of paper, to leave a great deal of margin. To embellish this copy he collected at a cost of £3300 more than 6000 engravings which were inserted in the text. This copy was bound in 45 volumes, and fitted into an elaborate oak case. Bowyer's daughter obtained 4000 guineas for it in a lottery. It was afterwards bought by John Albinson of Bolton — for a long time clerk to the Great Bolton Trust — and after his death sold by public auction and knocked down to Robert Heywood for £550. His grandsons gave it to Bolton Public Library, where it now occupies a considerable space in the foyer.

Throughout his life Robert Heywood belonged to small discussion groups, circulating round the members' houses, where papers were read and argued about, and sometimes there were play readings. Small societies of this kind have always been popular in Bolton and still flourish there. Before 1820 he was a regular attender at the Bolton Philosophical Society, to which he once read a paper on cotton. He took an interest in science. In 1818 he attended three lectures given in Bolton, at a charge of a guinea, by the great Manchester chemist John Dalton. For forty years he attended the annual meetings of the British Association for the Advancement of Science. He loved the theatre and concerts; one of the pleasures of travel for him was the opportunity to see and hear outstanding performances. At home he played the organ and made the most of visiting musicians and theatrical companies — at intervals some of the best actors of the day visited the Bolton Theatre.

One curious accidental link with an important man might be mentioned. One day in 1812, when Robert Heywood was walking past the Quaker Meeting House in Mealhouse Lane, he was asked inside to act as witness to a marriage — a runaway match between the parents of John Bright.

13

2. ENTRY INTO PUBLIC LIFE

In the early years of the nineteenth century and for many years to come, the handloom weavers were the most radical body of workers, and there was a large contingent in Bolton and the surrounding villages who had enjoyed great prosperity during the cotton boom which followed the invention of spinning machinery, but who found life harder and harder as the Napoleonic War continued. E.P.Thompson, in his book *The Making of the English Working Class,* says that to judge from Home Office records Bolton was one of the most disturbed towns in the kingdom, but concludes that this impression is mainly due to the vigilance and exaggerated reports of the local magistrates, particularly Ralph Fletcher, Colonel of the Bolton Light Horse Volunteers, a tireless defender of law and order and an extremist, who employed *agents provocateurs* to infiltrate into working class groups. The most sensational incident of this period was the destruction, during the Luddite disturbances of 1812, of a Westhoughton powerloom factory, for which several men and a boy were hanged.

Among the circle of Robert Heywood's close friends was Dr Robert Taylor, a trustee of Bank Street Chapel but a freethinker. Taylor brought forward evidence to show that Colonel Fletcher's spies had played a large part in provoking the attack at Westhoughton. For his services to the radical cause at this time Dr Taylor was presented with a hundred guineas' worth of plate. He is said to have been so disgusted with the repressive atmosphere of England that he emigrated to America immediately afterwards. There seems to be some confusion in this report. John Taylor, Robert's brother, had emigrated for the same reason at an earlier date, and it was John's grave in Poughkeepsie that Robert Heywood visited when he was in America in 1834. It is quite clear from the Heywood papers that a Dr Robert Taylor was still living in Bolton until the 1820's. The *Bolton Chronicle* recorded his death at Kaskaskia Illinois, in 1827.

During the next few years there was an atmosphere of class war in industrial Lancashire. Several societies existed aiming at the suppression of subversive radicalism, and on the other hand workers organized illegal unions and took part, sometimes peacefully and sometimes violently, in the movement for parliamentary reform after 1815.

Middle class Unitarians were more sympathetic to this radical movement than any other religious group, and more tolerant of the atheism of its extreme wing, represented by Tom Paine and Richard Carlile in England. Robert Heywood was clearly intensely interested in the writings of Paine and Carlile, but nowhere expresses his own views on them. He highly approved of William Cobbett, the denouncer of 'Bolton Fletcher', whose emigration to America in 1817 he regarded as 'an irreparable loss'. He had a furious dispute in that year with one of his oldest friends, S.D. Darbishire (a fellow Unitarian and the brother of Heywood's closest friend Charles Darbishire), about the merits of Dr Taylor. Heywood was provoked to write very rudely by Darbishire's criticisms of Dr Taylor, and called him a 'trimming timeserver' and a 'sneaking sycophant'. Heywood claimed that Dr. Taylor had exposed 'the most villainous system of espionage ever adopted by any government on the face of the earth'. Darbishire accused Taylor of fomenting violence, deplored his sceptical deism, and doubted whether he had made any real contribution to the exposure of a system which he also deplored. He allowed that the excellent constitution of the country might be improved, but 'not by the means the reformists recommend'. He admired men who gave the workers knowledge and material benefits, and not 'fantastical notions of liberty which they do not understand'. On the eve of Peterloo Unitarians were deeply divided in their attitudes to reform.

The Peterloo 'Massacre' occurred on 16th August 1819. A vast crowd of working people, swollen by large marching contingents from surrounding districts – including some from Bolton – assembled in St. Peter's Fields on the edge of Manchester to attend a meeting to be addressed by Henry Hunt, the rabble-rousing leader of the movement for parliamentary reform. Many of these marchers had been alarming the authorities by drilling. The meeting was entirely legal, held with a view to petitioning the Prince Regent against the Corn Laws and for the reform of Parliament. A special committee of Lancashire and Cheshire magistrates was set up to deal with the situation, and they chose as their chairman William Hulton of Hulton Park near Bolton, the youngest of the magistrates and a close friend of Colonel Fletcher, who was also present as a member of the committee.

The magistrates viewed the proceedings from the upper room of a house which overlooked St. Peter's Fields. The Manchester Yeomanry, a body of enthusiastic amateur partisans, had been assembled to help to maintain order, and these were backed by some companies of regular soldiers, who were, however, not present when Hunt and the other speakers mounted the hustings to address the vast concourse. The magistrates had decided on the arrest of Hunt and several other leaders, and they used the Yeomanry to make the arrests. Whether the Yeomanry was attacked or merely obstructed is still not certain, but they set about the crowd surrounding them. Seeing the tumult Hulton ordered a company of Hussars which had just arrived to rescue the Yeomanry, effect the arrests, and clear the whole space. Colonel Fletcher rushed in, hitting people with his cane. The soldiers rapidly dispersed the crowd, the arrests were made, and in the melée seven people were killed and several hundred injured. (See R. Walmsley: *Peterloo, the Case Reopened*, for an exhaustive new treatment of the subject and an assessment favourable to the authorities.)

Meetings of protest were held all over the country after this event, and the Bolton radicals planned to hold one in the New Market Place, but in view of the hostility of the local division of the county magistrates they decided that they would meet in Dr Taylor's field in Moor Lane. The intended meeting was respectably sponsored by William Bowker, the Unitarian who, by some aberration of the Court Leet, had been appointed Boroughreeve of Great Bolton for that year; he was supported by 27 middle-class householders, many of them members of Bank

Street.   John Heywood, not as a rule politically active, was one of these, and Robert appears to have acted as a kind of secretary, for there is a draft in his hand of a number of resolutions to be proposed, with various alterations. He drafted a letter for circulation to the public that shows the origin of this middle-class leadership: 'Knowing that the people were resolved to have a meeting to express their sentiments and finding the higher and most of the middle class as usual unwilling to come forward we were induced to step forward.'

Because their own magistrates had been in the forefront at Peterloo, the Bolton protesters expected unfair treatment, and took the extraordinary step of writing to J.A. Borron, the chairman of the Warrington magistrates, whom they regarded as a sympathizer, to ask for protection. Their letter reads:

'It may be known to some of you that the inhabitants of the towns of Great and Little Bolton and Neighbourhood intend to exercise a legal and constitutional right of meeting publicly to address the Prince Regent on the late proceedings at Manchester on the 16th of August last.   That in consequence of the measures pursued on that much-to-be-lamented occasion by some of the Magistrates of this Division and their subsequent conduct in trampling upon the rights of the people we the undersigned request your attendance to protect the people while in the exercise of their constitutional rights, being convinced that it is unsafe to assemble without your protection.'

Borron replied that 'unless the apprehensions you seemed to express should appear to be well founded, a circumstance I should be extremely unwilling to admit, any interference on my part would be highly indecorous and improper'. He had, however, decided to consult Lord Derby, the Lord Lieutenant, who replied:

'As you have laid this business before me expressing in some degree a wish that I should interfere in it, I have thought it my duty to lay the business before the magistrates specially acting for the Bolton division, only stating that it confirmed me in the opinion which I had before ventured to express to them: That the subject had a constitutional and legal right to assemble for the purpose of stating to the Crown or Parliament or expressing publicly their opinion upon any public question or supposed grievance, and that as long as they conducted themselves peaceably and without any infringement of the laws of the Realm they could not legally be interrupted in this exercise by any authority whatsoever.   I can have no objection to these sentiments being communicated to the gentlemen who have applied to you but at the same time I can give no sort of pledge that their intended meeting shall not be interrupted by the magistrates, with whom I can never think myself called upon or justified to interpose in the discretionary exercise of the power and authority intrusted to them by law.'

Borron sent them a copy of Lord Derby's letter, and advised against holding the meeting. 'In the present irritated state of the public mind, it might be attended with very dangerous consequences.'   It was in fact believed by the magistrates that pikes had been made in Leigh, and that trouble-makers from there intended to go to the Bolton meeting.

The organizers went ahead with their plans, and the magistrates issued a public notice cautioning the people against attending. The radicals countered with a notice enjoining 'on all persons attending the said meeting the indispensable necessity of conducting themselves in the most orderly and peaceable manner, and should the least insult or outrage be offered by their designing enemies, they are *particularly urged* not to resent the same but to take such notice of the offenders that they may be brought to justice on a future day.'

The resolutions intended for the Prince Regent asserted their consitutional rights, and claimed 'that the public meeting at Manchester on the 16th of August was a lawful meeting; that from every inquiry we have made, its proceedings were conducted in a peaceable and orderly manner, that......the people......were wantonly, wickedly and brutally attacked by an armed force of men called Yeomanry Cavalry aided and encouraged by the local magistrates, and that men, women and children were indiscriminately slaughtered by those infamous ruffians.' To them it seemed 'that this disgraceful occurrence......is a developing part of the execrable system so long practised in this immediate neighbourhood.' They thought that 'one lamentable consequence has been the loss of all confidence in the laws of the realm', and 'that the thanks of the Regent on this occasion have identified his advisers with the guilty perpetrators of this foul deed.' The only acceptable solution was 'the radical reform of the Commons house as the only guardian of the people's rights and the best security against military despotism.' Henry Hunt they commended as the hero of the occasion. They proposed a subscription to relieve the sufferers and to bring the perpetrators to justice.

The local magistrates eventually used their discretionary powers to ban this meeting, and it was abandoned. As soon as Parliament met, new laws – the Six Acts, sometimes called the Gagging Acts – were passed, which made all such meetings illegal, and made outspoken opposition very dangerous.

The resolutions quoted above show how quickly the radical myth of Peterloo was established. We have to turn to the proceedings of such bodies as the Bolton Pitt Club to find the Tory myth. At their annual dinner at the Commercial Inn in 1820, attended by the Vicar and most of the leading townsmen of Bolton, they toasted 'Mr Hulton and the Committee of Magistrates of Manchester and the neighbourhood who successfully exerted themselves in the discharge of their duty for the preservation of their country.' So the bad judgment and panicky behaviour of the Peterloo magistrates was elevated into heroism. The most extreme outbursts of this kind of patriotism were to be found at the annual birthday dinners in honour of Colonel Fletcher, which were even continued after his death as a memorial tribute. The gulf between parties was very wide and deep.

Robert Heywood did more to bridge this gap than any other Bolton radical of his generation. Passionately involved at the time of Peterloo, he mellowed without ever abandoning his liberal outlook. His two abiding interests were the democratization of government and the creation of a better environment for the people of Bolton, and in the pursuit of the latter aim he forgot all political and religious animosities.

The first example of this is his work for the Bolton Dispensary which he helped to found and of which he was secretary from its beginning in 1813 until his death in 1868. In 1825 it moved from its original premises in Mawdsley Street to a pleasant classical stone-fronted building in Nelson Square designed by the famous local engineer Benjamin Hick, which also provided accommodation for patients in an infirmary. To help to pay for this building Heywood organized a bazaar in the parish church schoolroom at which Mrs William Hulton presided over a stall, and which raised £700. The Dispensary and Infirmary employed one house surgeon, paid in 1837 £100 a year. It must always have been very inadequate to the needs of a rapidly growing, disease-ridden industrial town. When in 1837 the committee decided to add two wings to the building, Heywood headed the donation list and a little later doubled his annual subscription. But it was a very modest affair; in 1842 the total annual expenditure was only £455 – for a population of 70,000 – and the enlarged building was not fully used, the new north wing being let for a time as a private house. The Vicar of Bolton, Rev. J. Slade (later Canon Slade) was chairman of the Dispensary Committee for much of the time Heywood was secretary, and they struck up a friendship across political and religious barriers. When Heywood was ill the Vicar visited him regularly.

Another venture in which Heywood participated was the estabishment of the Exchange News Room, of which he was one of the founders in 1813. Newspapers at sevenpence a copy – of which sixpence was tax – were an expensive commodity, and members of the society were glad to pay an annual subscription for the privilege of dropping in to read the Manchester, Liverpool and London papers. For several years they had the use of a room at the Commercial Inn. Heywood himself visited the newsroom nearly every day, and he soon became the secretary. In 1817 he wrote a letter answering a charge of political bias in the choice of newspapers, in which he claimed that as an official he had regarded himself as a trustee for the general good, regardless of his personal views.

By 1824 the committee was ready to build. They commissioned Richard Lane, the leading Manchester architect of the time and the master of Alfred Waterhouse, to design for them a classical building in the New Market Place – now Victoria Square – where it still stands, looking across to their earlier home in the Commercial Hotel. When the building was completed in 1826 they decided to form a library, for which there was to be a subscription of one guinea a year. At this time there were more than 300 subscribers to the news room. The financial burden was considerable, much of it borne by Heywood, and a letter from him in the *Bolton Free Press* in 1835 pointed out that £4000 had been spent and that the shareholders had received only one ten shilling dividend. At this time it was decided that the library subscription should be reduced to 10/- per annum and that for library and newsroom combined the subscription should be 30/-   The next year membership became open to all without restriction. Eventually the building was taken over by the Corporation, and for many years housed the Reference Library.

A far more urgent problem in Bolton than the enlightenment of the middle class was the provision of educational facilities for working men and children. From its beginning in 1825 Robert Heywood supported and subscribed to the Bolton Mechanics' Institution, of which his friend Charles Darbishire was the secretary for many years; he was a member of its first committee, a trustee from 1833, and president in 1852-3.

Although there was no overt political activity in the Mechanics' Institution – it was even supported by a handful of conservatives – there were frequent accusations of bias and the indoctrination of working men. William Cobbett gave four lectures to the Mechanics in 1830 which were pungently partisan. In 1831 the members were very legitimately asked to sign a petition against the newspaper duty of 6d per copy, which made them too dear for the working man, and Heywood himself presented this petition to the House of Commons. When Lord Brougham, the founder of the movement for the education of working men, visited Bolton in 1835, he spoke strongly against the 'taxes on knowledge'. In February 1836 Heywood took the chair at a public meeting on this question held in the theatre, a new experience for him, and he trusted they would forgive his imperfections, as it was his first appearance on these boards. The outcome was another petition to Parliament. The campaign was partly successful, for later in the year Melbourne's government reduced the newspaper duty to 3d.

The Mechanics' Institution provided a reading room and organized a number of classes, at one time criticized by Heywood as too much directed to juvenile needs. They included a class in mechanical drawing taught by Darbishire, and a much more popular drawing and painting class taught by the local artist Selim Rothwell, once himself a prizewinner at the Mechanics' Institution. Rev. Franklin Baker once unsuccessfully opposed a class in mathematics on the remarkable ground that it was a subject which added nothing to the happiness of mankind. Public lectures were organized from time to time, at which the general public paid for admission but members were admitted free.   In 1837 Heywood paid the costs of a series of lectures on phrenology, a fashionable pseudo-science. The borough coroner gave monologue readings from Shakespeare, a whole play in an evening.   In 1846 a working man gave a lecture on Shakespeare, which according to the *Free Press* evinced no ordinary degree of ability for a person of his class'.   The library of over 2000 volumes was said in 1840 to be 'by far the most valuable in the town to which the public have access'.

The membership of the Mechanics' Institution remained obstinately small. About 120 joined in 1825, and the numbers of active members rarely exceeded 200.   The society did not grow with the growth of the town. The rooms they met in were described as dull and cheerless, and members wrote to the paper complaining that they could not read for the noise of the classes. Heywood helped them to move to new premises in 1838, but he felt that the society was too sectarian, and that much wider support was wanted. At the annual meeting in 1845 Charles Darbishire resigned the secretaryship, in part because of allegations of bias, and a conservative friend of Heywood's, T.R. Bridson the bleacher, became committee chairman. The next year Heywood sponsored a widely supported meeting, with John Hick, a leading conservative and chairman of the engineering firm of Benjamin Hick and Son, in the chair, to found an 'Atheneum' for working men to absorb the Mechanics' Institution, a well meant attempt that failed.

Edmund Ashworth gave a paper to the British Association in 1837 giving the results of a survey he had made of education in Bolton. According to him Bolton had the worst record of any town in the country, with only 2500 children attending day schools. His figures were challenged, and it was asserted that 3200 attended day or evening schools, 7800 had Sunday School instruction only, and 3489 children between the ages of five and fifteen were entirely uneducated. No one who was a radical and a democrat could remain unconcerned about this problem. Heywood did all he could through Sunday School work. He advocated a national scheme of secular education that was a non-starter in Victorian conditions, though he opposed any plan for public aid that included assistance to Anglican schools — until the 1870 compromise was reached, this issue bedevilled all attempts at a national system. He also supported voluntary schemes. He was a donor and founder trustee of the British School in All Saints Street, Little Bolton, founded in 1835 — a school that soon won high praise for good results and enlightened methods, including the virtual abolition of corporal punishment. He was a trustee of the Hulton Charity which set up a day school in Moor Lane. Later in life he helped to found the Certified Industrial School in Commission Street.

Robert Heywood was drawn fully into the management of public affairs in Bolton when he was appointed a Trustee of Great Bolton in 1826. Local authority was divided between the old village government by the Court Leet and its officials, the county magistrates, and the improvement trusts. Great and Little Bolton each had a Court Leet held by the lords of the manors once a year, at which a boroughreeve, two constables and various lesser officials were appointed to manage the townships. Much of the work of local government fell upon the Bolton division of the county magistrates, who appointed the overseers of the poor, supervised the maintenance of law and order by the boroughreeves, and licensed inns and alehouses. In 1792 Parliament passed an act for the enclosure of Bolton Moor, belonging to Great Bolton. Commissioners were appointed to sell the land in lots subject to an annual ground rent. This income was then to be used to aid the poor rates and for 'widening, paving, lighting, watching, cleansing and watering the streets, and for providing fire engines and firemen, and for removing and preventing annoyances in the said town of Great Bolton'. Trustees, 41 in number, were set up to administer this Act, which also established a trust for Little Bolton with 30 Trustees with the same powers but no income from rents. Both Trusts had power to levy a rate — usually called the police rate.

So these 'large, populous and trading towns, and daily increasing', received their first municipal government. The Trustees were appointed for life, and vacancies were filled by cooption; in Great Bolton they had to be worth £1000 in real or personal property, in Little Bolton £500. They met in secret, and very little of what went on at their meetings was ever revealed to the public, even when a local press came into existence. (Volumes I and III of the Records of the Great Bolton Trust are deposited in the Bolton borough archives. Volume II is in the Reference Library.) On the whole they dovetailed into the existing establishment, though some nonconformists were included in the first list — one of the Great Bolton Trustees was Joseph McKeand, a cotton merchant and Unitarian, whose son married Robert Heywood's sister.

The smallness of the income from the Moor, about £2500 a year, and the hostility of the ratepayers to levies on top of the poor rate (a heavy charge in times of bad trade) hampered the efforts of the Trustees of Great Bolton to improve the town, but they provided a workhouse and a primitive fire service manned for some years by volunteers, and it is to their credit that some of the main streets leading from the town centre are a good width, and above all that Victoria Square exists. This was the New Market Place, laid out to get the market stalls out of the blocked main streets. In 1819 the Trustees made a contract with the Bolton Gas Company — whose directors were mainly Trustees — to light the town streets with gas. They attacked the growing problem of sanitation by contracting with farmers for the removal of night soil, and from this they obtained an income of £30 a year. They did their best to prevent the pollution of wells, and Bolton was fortunate in having a very early supply of water from a distance, when a Waterworks Company, set up by Act of Parliament in 1823, again largely directed by Trustees, obtained a supply of water from a reservoir at Belmont in the moors to the north of the town.

The circumstances of Robert Heywood's election in 1826 are unknown. He had moved with his family from Little Bolton to Great Bolton in 1824 when his father took a new terraced house with seven bedrooms in Newport Terrace, Manchester Road, a site now occupied by a British Rail goods warehouse. Heywood was away on his first long trip abroad when he was elected as one of four new Trustees, one other of whom, Thomas Gregson, was likewise a cotton manufacturer and a liberal. It may well be that the disturbed state of the town in that year of slump and unrest induced the Trustees to elect liberals.

Of the forty Trustees the majority attended very irregularly or not at all. Robert Heywood was a fairly consistent attender at meetings varying from five to twenty-five in number, and soon became important because of his insistence on honest and businesslike proceedings. It is clear that he was quickly accepted by his fellow Trustees although they nearly all differed from him politically. A chairman was elected at each meeting, and Heywood was frequently elected. He played a very active part in securing the removal of encroachments from the street footpaths, which were to be at least four feet wide without obstruction. More important, he attacked the abuses which nearly always crept into the administration of such bodies; in 1828 he carried a motion that all work and materials wanted by the Trust should be publicly contracted for.

The respect in which he was held was shown when in December 1831 he was elected Treasurer of the Trust, an office he held for twelve years. He insisted on the publication of the accounts, and they now appeared annually in the local papers. The Trustees had run into debt rather than levy rates for all their expenses, and owed about £10,000, mainly to the Fletcher family, some of it at too high a rate of interest. Heywood obtained powers to repay all loans borrowed at more than 4% and proposed economies, especially in the lighting of the streets by gas — to be discontinued in summer and to be only during 'the dark of the moon' for the rest of the year. He disliked the private monopolies of gas and water, largely controlled by fellow Trustees, and always thought that they cost too much.

One of Heywood's main interests in the Trust was the improvement of the rudimentary fire service. He served on the Fire Brigade Committee from its inception in 1827. In 1836 he persuaded the Trustees to set up a full time uniformed force of sixteen men with a superintendent. Fortunately the biggest cotton mills had their own fire engines, and sent these to help the fire brigade at serious fires. There were eventually four fire engines belonging to the Trust, Bumble, Jesse, Blucher and Globe.

Without sacrificing his basic convictions Robert Heywood had become an accepted public figure. When he was given the treasurership the *Bolton Chronicle* complimented him: 'We doubt not, from the high character he has hitherto held, that he will perform the duties, which are entirely gratuitous, with profit to the town and honour to himself.' He was notably silent at public meetings, a seconder of resolutions. His laconic style when he had to speak became a joke in the town. But behind the scenes he was now listened to and held in honour. He took the chair at four out of seven critical Trust meetings in 1831.

3. THE REFORMING THIRTIES

Reform in Bolton began, not with the Reform Bill of 1830, but with some Poor Law reforms initiated by William Naisby, a Scots draper with a shop in Hotel Street. The severe slump of 1826 was felt all the more in Bolton because calico weavers were already suffering from the competition of power looms. The poor rate for Great Bolton rose to 15/- in the £ in 1827. Naisby refused to pay his rates and held protest meetings. He alleged that the administration by the Overseers was so bad that less than half the proceeds went to the relief of the poor. His demand for the reduction of the salaries paid to various officals from £1000 to £380 was unreasonable, but popular with his audiences − when the rate was halved later on he demanded the halving of the salary of the collector. Much more justified was his criticism of the assessments, which favoured the rich, and he forced the magistrates to revise these. He also secured the first democratic reform in the history of Bolton, by winning the concession that the magistrates would allow the ratepayers of Great Bolton to elect, in a meeting usually presided over by the vicar, nominees for the posts of Overseers of the Poor and Surveyors of Highways, from whom they would normally make their appointments. Liberals soon won their share − or more − of office as Naisby packed the meetings, and they greatly reduced costs, not entirely at the expense of the poor. Robert Heywood, Overseer of the Poor in 1833-4, was one of these.

In 1829 a public announcement appeared in the *Bolton Chronicle* of a plan for reorganizing the Great Bolton Trust and making it representative. The agent, and possibly the principal, in this scheme was Ralph Boardman, Town Clerk and formerly Solicitor to the Trust, from which he was alleged to have obtained £14,000 all told in fees. In the end, after two public meetings had been held, this plan was rejected as bogus by both conservatives and liberals. The whole affair is most obscure. Robert Heywood, who wanted the townspeople to have more say in their own affairs, was a leader in the opposition. In the end there was no legislative reform of the Great Bolton Trust, but in 1830 an Act of Parliament reformed the Little Bolton Trust by providing for the election of the Trustees in a public meeting of ratepayers.

The Great Bolton Trustees did however try out a reformed method of appointment, a short-lived experiment which had the strongest support of Robert Heywood. The Great Bolton ratepayers' meetings already played a considerable part in the government of the township. They not only had some voice in the appointment of Overseers and Surveyors but also discussed and voted upon their accounts and those of the Constables. In 1831 the Trustees decided that when there was a vacancy in the Trust it should be filled from four nominees elected at a ratepayers' meeting announced by the town bellman. This cautious experiment in representation, which was inaugurated during the excitements of the first Reform Bill, was abandoned after two years. William Naisby's well-drilled radical group was too successful. Of six Trustees elected by the new procedure five were certainly radicals, and one even had the audacity to propose that a reporter should be admitted to meetings of the Trust! In March 1833 the Trustees called a halt. They ignored the ratepayers' nominees by a vote of fifteen to twelve, and neither Heywood nor any other liberal or radical Trustee signed the minutes. The next time there was a vacancy they decided by twelve votes to eight not to call a meeting. One radical Trustee resigned in protest. For some years Heywood did not sign the minutes when there was a Trustee appointment, and he was still trying in 1837 for a revival of ratepayers' meetings, but had only two supporters. The Trust had drawn back into its shell.

Robert Heywood had stood firmly with the radicals on this issue and they were not ungrateful. At a ratepayers' meeting in 1837, where he had persuaded the radicals to take a moderate course about some disputed accounts, Naisby said: 'We all know that gentleman as a friend of the people.'

Politics in Bolton took fire with the introduction of the Reform Bill in 1830. The 'county' society – the anciently established Hultons of Hulton, the coalowning Fletchers, and pseudo-gentry such as Joseph Ridgway, the Horwich bleacher who once challenged a magistrate's clerk to a duel – were so much antagonized by William IV's apparent support for reform that they boycotted the King's birthday dinner in 1831. Only one magistrate and one clergyman took part in an event which had traditionally been the occasion for the enthusiastic demonstration of extreme tory views. On the other hand some of the conservative businessmen, such as the bleachers James Hardcastle and Stephen Blair – a later conservative M.P. for the borough – supported the Bill. The middle class reformers, mainly nonconformists led by Bank Street Unitarians, were democrats who accepted the bill with enthusiasm as an instalment, but continued to demand household suffrage and the ballot. This and their selective support of working class causes kept them in touch with more radical groups. Heywood supported the anti-truck campaign which was being vigorously pushed at this time, he opposed the newspaper tax, and he strongly supported the campaign for shorter working hours in mills. He and even more his friend Charles Darbishire maintained links with Naisby and his radicals.

Working class politics in Bolton were exceptionally complex in the 1830's, because in addition to the workers in mills, bleachworks and engineering shops, and the builders and labourers, there was one of the largest remaining bodies of handloom weavers, mainly men engaged in skilled work in the fancy cotton trade, Bolton's speciality. There were fewer power looms than elsewhere in South Lancashire, as so far they were incapable of producing fancy textiles, but there was an excess of weavers and severe depression, especially in 1837 and from 1839 to 1842, when Bolton experienced as much misery and starvation as anywhere in England. (Dr. D. Bythell's recent book on *The Handloom Weavers* is indispensable to a knowledge of the background of this situation.) In spite of this there was less violence than in many other towns in the political upheavals of the time, and this may have been due, as Dr Bythell suggests, to the apathetic despair of many weavers, but there were vigorous efforts to involve the workers in middle class political activities, which both divided and tamed the politically alert. At the time of the introduction of the Reform Bill the more extreme working men attended meetings held from time to time in Bradford Square and addressed by John Doherty, the outstanding Manchester trade unionist. For a time he worked closely with Henry Hunt (M.P. for Preston in 1831), and they put forward approximately the programme of demands later incorporated in the People's Charter. Naisby's radical group linked up with them, and together they formed a Bolton Political Union in 1830, which held a big public meeting in the Theatre in November.

In the critical spring of 1831 Robert Heywood and his friends worked for unity in the reform movement. At a great public meeting in February Blair and Hardcastle joined Charles Darbishire and Rev. Franklin Baker in supporting the bill introduced by Lord John Russell, but a splitting radical amendment in favour of manhood suffrage and vote by ballot was carried. A petition to Parliament that arose out of this meeting was signed by 10,000 people in three days. At the next meeting, where Heywood proposed a resolution thanking Russell, Franklin Baker overcame working class opposition with a powerful plea for unity in the cause. A number of working men spoke in support, and hoped that the middle classes would come to their help later. The first bill allocated only one M.P. to Bolton, and a memorial was now sent to the Prime Minister pointing out that the population of Great and Little Bolton was over 43,000 and asking for two M.P.'s, a plea that was granted in the final bill. The Bolton Political Union, influenced by speeches from Hunt and Doherty, decided to oppose the bill as a measure of no use to the workers, but Naisby supported it as a useful half measure, and he and his friends left the Union. The extremists were few.

When the first election was held in Bolton in December 1832 four candidates stood for the two seats. The tories put up William Bolling, an important local cotton spinner. The whig candidate, fairly radical, was Colonel Robert Torrens, who had been a member for a disfranchised borough; he was quite well known as a writer on economic questions. The Bolton liberals were prepared to support him, but brought forward their own candidate, a reforming Unitarian Councillor from Liverpool, J.A. Yates. The radicals had some difficulty in finding anyone to stand, but at the last minute produced a candidate in William Eagle. Torrens headed the poll, and Bolling beat Yates for second place by ten votes. Eagle had only 107 votes. (Heywood voted for Torrens and Yates.) Bolling stirred up a great deal of local loyalty, and began a tradition of Bolton electing local men which has not yet died — only between 1945 and 1950 was Bolton without at least one Bolton man among its two M.P.'s. Bolling's procession on polling day was very impressive. He set out from his house, Darcy Lever Hall, in a carriage drawn by greys, and at Haulgh Hall bridge was joined by a large contingent of gentlemen on horseback, all the bands the town could muster, most of the local friendly society lodges, and squads of workers, mainly women and girls from his own and a number of other mills in the town. There was a riot when this procession reached the New Market Place, and radical non-voters prevented Bolling from being heard, although their leaders appealed to them to give him a hearing. The magistrates read the Riot Act and called out the troops to quell the mob. At the declaration of the poll the victorious Colonel Torrens was struck by a stone and incapacitated for several days. His opponents accused Bolling of winning votes by wholesale treating, but compared with the elections in many old-established boroughs it was all good clean fun. There was no organized thuggery as at Coventry nor universal bribery as at Hatfield.

At this time Heywood worked mainly in the background of politics. He was very conscious of the fact that most of the money in Bolton belonged to tories, and he contributed generously to campaign funds. When the *Bolton Chronicle* abandoned the liberal cause, he subsidized the new liberal paper, the *Bolton Free Press*. When Lord Molyneux of Sefton was the whig candidate for South Lancashire in the January 1835 election, Heywood was chairman of his Bolton committee. (Owners of freeholds and large leaseholders in Bolton had county as well as borough votes.) Heywood wrote to Molyneux's agent a letter that reveals something of the nature of county campaigns at that time. 'Tomorrow I purpose riding over to see Mr Green, though we have little expectation from the Hultons [Little, Middle and Over Hulton] as they are almost entirely under the influence of Egerton and Hulton. Many of the electors in Bradshaw unfortunately are employed by Hardcastle and have been early canvassed under that interest. Those of Great Lever Farnworth and Tonge are mostly tenants and forced to vote agreeably to the wishes of Lord Bradford. Rumworth and Heaton [largely owned by the whig Mrs Tempest] we consider pretty safe. We wish the same could be said of Horwich and Lostock largely owned by Mr Stonor, whose agent is a furious tory resorting to all the tricks of that party, and we fear hardly to be trusted even if Mr Stonor should prove favourable. Blackrod is a poor place, most of the votes promised to Mr Ridgway for Lord Egerton, and we fear there will be great difficulty in getting even any of the splits for want of some really active person in the neighbourhood to look after them and bring them up.'

At this election Peter Ainsworth — the bleacher who had acquired and enlarged Smithills Hall, the finest of Bolton's old houses — was the second reform candidate in Bolton. Bolling headed the poll, Ainsworth was second, and Torrens the outsider did very badly. It was a quiet election. The Poor Law Amendment Act, enacted by the Whig Government in 1834, had embarrassed the liberals and heartened the conservatives. It showed the gulf between middle class liberals and the working class. The intention of the Poor Law Commissioners to impose a workhouse test appalled the workers and their radical leaders. The imposition of Poor Law Commissioners to enforce the will of the central authority on local elected Boards of Guardians offended all parties. Brandreth, a Bank Street radical, called it the work of 'Malthusian system-mongers'. Moderate liberals reserved judgment. When Robert Heywood was in America in 1834 his friend Charles Darbishire wrote to him: 'There were meetings called lately by the overseers both in Great and Little Bolton for the purpose of declaiming against the new poor bill — factious meetings I call them, got up by the officials because there will now be a power above them which they cannot cajole. I attended the Little Bolton meeting and defended the bill.' Somewhat later, at an early meeting of the Bolton Guardians, Heywood said that 'he certainly did object to some of the clauses, but he thought the bill was such that the Guardians might, if they chose, put it into effect with considerable benefit to the Union'.

Disillusionment with the reformed Parliament and above all with the new Poor Law provided a great opportunity for the conservatives to rally support among the workers, and they did not neglect it. Another issue actively taken up by Bolton conservatives was that of handloom weavers' wages. In 1834 a joint committee of manufacturers and weavers promoted a petition for the regulation of wages locally — the main objection was to cut-rate manufacturers who paid lower wages than the current agreed scale. Neither Robert Heywood nor Charles Darbishire was a member of this committee, and it is obvious that, like many of the weavers themselves, they had no faith in regulation to prevent malpractices. The leading manufacturers were John Makin and Thomas Myerscough, manager of a handloom weaving shop, an able man but rather a maverick in politics, who began as an awkward radical and eventually became a conservative Mayor of Bolton. The chief weavers' representatives were Richard Needham and Philip Halliwell. These two and Makin were basically conservative in outlook, but they had considerable liberal and radical support, and in March 1834 Torrens, strongly supported by Bolling, presented three petitions, one from the weavers, one from the manufacturers, and one from the magistrates and clergy of Bolton, which resulted in the setting up of a select committee of inquiry (see D. Bythell: *The Handloom Weavers* p.160).

The next year John Maxwell brought in a bill for establishing local boards of trade of manufacturers and weavers to fix wages. Bolling supported him, but Ainsworth, the new liberal M.P., objected to a clause for taxing power looms, and abstained from voting. In Bolton the weavers were very evenly split for and against the Bill. When it was defeated in the House of Commons three acrimonious meetings of weavers were held in Bolton within a fortnight. At the first two meetings radical weavers, some of whom were Chartists later on, carried the day against the Bill and the Bolton Weavers' Committee, but at the third Needham obtained a majority for the Bill. Philip Halliwell, his chief supporter among the weavers, refused a place on the committee of the South Lancashire Conservative Association on the grounds that he had no vote. At this point William Hulton advocated a separate organization for working class conservatives.

A recent book (R. Walmsley: *Peterloo, the Case Reopened)* has vindicated William Hulton from the worst of the Peterloo charges. He had exerted himself for the workers by active lobbying for anti-truck legislation, and more recently for the Bill to regulate weavers' wages. He had considerable influence, especially in the House of Lords with the extreme Church and King tories, and the Weavers' Committee thanked him for his services. Now, on his suggestion and with the full financial backing of the Bolling interest, the Bolton Operative Conservative Association was formed in November 1835, with Philip Halliwell as one of its leading sponsors. It soon had several hundred members, to the alarm and disgust of the liberals. Heywood wrote an indignant letter to the *Bolton Free Press* alleging that the members were bribed by subsidized dinners and abundant supplies of liquor; but the Association had a genuine basis in fear of the whig Poor Law and resentment at the lack of reforms of benefit to the working man. Before the 1837 election the Operative Conservatives held a grand dinner in a temporary building erected by their rich friends for the purpose. The decorations included numerous flags and banners and a picture of the storming of Seringapatam, painted on 2000 square feet of canvas by a local artist, Baxendale. Over a thousand dined, and two hundred ladies occupied the gallery — whether they also dined is not clear. The chair, in front of which was placed a gilt crown and a Bible, was occupied by Foster, the editor of the *Bolton Chronicle*.

The liberals of Bolton made their own moves to attract working men. In August 1835 they organized a public dinner of non-electors in honour of Peter Ainsworth. At a meeting of weavers held in Nelson Square during the depression, a majority demanded the repeal of the Corn Laws, about to become the favourite liberal remedy for poverty. The constitution of the Bolton Reform Association, formed in the same year, laid it down that twelve of the thirty-six members of the committee must be non-electors. Membership had the attraction for working men of access to a reading room stocked with books and newspapers. The Association had a strongly radical outlook — William Naisby was on the committee — and supported household suffrage and the ballot. The first president was Henry Ashworth, the Quaker millowner, one of two brothers who were to play a big part in Bolton politics in the ensuing years. Charles Darbishire succeeded him in 1838. Robert Heywood was not at first on the committee, though later he was a member for many years. At the first meeting he spoke forcibly about local issues, the inadequacy of the local police and the need for incorporation.

While the political parties in Bolton were competing for working class support, the Chartist movement had begun as a reaction against middle class tutelage and middle class reform. Henry Hetherington of the London Working Men's Association spoke in Bolton in November 1837. He brought forward the programme later embodied in the People's Charter, attacked the Bolton Reform Association as a middle class fraud, and proposed the formation of a local association of working men. Naisby said that one had existed in the past, and he had left it because it advocated the calling of a National Convention, which he described as 'treasonable'.

There was considerable Chartist activity in Bolton in 1838. Feargus O'Connor, the fiery editor of the Leeds *Northern Star*, gave a lecture in February. The People's Charter was strongly approved by the *Bolton Free Press*, which means that middle class liberals were friendly to the aims of the movement. William Naisby took the chair at a Chartist public meeting in September. George Lloyd, a joiner who was to be a leader in the troubles the next year, proposed the main resolution, but he was seconded by Thomas Thomasson, and Charles Darbishire and P.R. Arrowsmith spoke in support. Thomasson and Arrowsmith were wealthy cotton spinners, later prominent in the Anti-Corn Law League. The liberal leaders took no part in a torchlight procession in November in honour of Feargus O'Connor, the rabble rouser; O'Connor claimed a crowd of 50,000, more than the entire population of Bolton! The more modest local estimate was 10,000. In February 1839 the Bolton Chartists chose Joseph Wood, a tea dealer, to be their representative in the National Convention, and at this point they still had the support of Naisby (who had changed his mind about the Convention), Arrowsmith and Thomasson. They all soon withdrew when the talk became more violent. Wood resigned, and Gillespie, a working man, took his place.

Bolton liberals were in the forefront at this very time in launching the Anti-Corn Law campaign advocated by Richard Cobden, but for the moment they made little impression on the working man. The first big public meeting held in July 1838 was notable for the emergence of A.W. Paulton, a Bolton medical student who made a brilliant speech which attracted Cobden's notice. Paulton eventually became one of the chief paid propagandists of the Anti-Corn Law League. The Ashworths and Darbishire took the lead in forming a local Anti-Corn Law Association in January 1839, and Robert Heywood was one of a deputation sent to meet the central board, at this time in London. A meeting in February, when the Chartist excitement was at its height, was very crowded and disorderly, and Darbishire had a difficult time in the chair. A large section of the meeting was present in order to carry Chartist resolutions, and the proceedings broke up in disorder. The leadership of the Chartists in Bolton had passed into the hands of working men, Lloyd and Warden, who regarded the Anti-Corn Law movement as a middle class trick to cheat the workers.

4. THE BOLTON CORPORATION AND THE CHARTISTS

Robert Heywood was exceptional among the liberals of Bolton in his involvement in local public affairs.   He was concerned about national questions, as we have seen, and an active politician, but the welfare of Bolton always came first with him. As a Great Bolton Trustee and Secretary of the Dispensary he gained much experience of the day-to-day problems of the town, and his year as Overseer of the Poor had confronted him with the overwhelming poverty.   He must have been very much aware of the large share of his own industry of hand loom manufacturing in creating poverty in Bolton, but nowhere in his extant papers does he refer to this, except in general comments on the state of trade.   For improvement he pinned his faith to the abolition of private and privileged monopolies, better education, the extension of democratic public control, and philanthropy, hopelessly inadequate as that was bound to be.

In September 1835 Heywood received his appointment as a county magistrate, the first Bolton liberal to be appointed.   The office carried great responsibilities. The magistrates meeting in General Sessions at Preston controlled the local government of Lancashire as a whole; the local magistrates were responsible for law and order and for the efficient performance of their duties by all the local officials, and especially the Overseers of the Poor.   A variable number sat on the bench at the Bolton Petty Sessions, held once or twice a week.   At first Heywood was a diffident magistrate.   Within a few weeks of his appointment he found himself alone on the bench one day with some difficult cases, and deferred them all because of his limited experience;   for this action he was criticized in the local press.   As he became more at home he became noted for his humour and shrewdness, and for a desire to avoid convictions for petty offences.   Many a drunk escaped by a promise to take the teetotal pledge.

Robert Heywood's new public position gave him a high status among the reformers, and he was much in demand at public meetings.   But his first recorded public speech was made just before his appointment, at a public meeting called to discuss the Municipal Corporations Bill of 1835, and to petition the Lords to pass it without amendments.   Heywood said he was 'no great speechifier'; he attacked the corrupt close corporations, Liverpool and East Retford being examples.   He knew a man who had been a councillor at East Retford, and found that 'all he had to do for the East Retford corporation was to dine sumptuously to the enlargement of his own.'   He criticized the Great Bolton Trust as an unrepresentative body, and hoped that this Bill would place the power in worthier hands.   Naisby and Myerscough attacked a clause in the Bill which would leave trusts the option of continuing in existence after a new corporation was set up, but the M.P. Peter Ainsworth said it would be impossible in the existing temper of the House of Commons to carry a clause making compulsory the winding up of improvement trusts.

From this time on the reformers in Bolton looked forward to a charter of incorporation. (In this chapter there is a risk of confusion between this local charter and the People's Charter demanded nationally at the same time by the Chartists. The latter will be referred to by its full title.) At meetings to win radical support in 1837 Robert Heywood repeatedly urged action to secure a charter of incorporation. Henry Ashworth, in his *Recollections of Richard Cobden*, tells of the first steps taken to obtain this, at the same time as Cobden was active in a similar movement in Manchester. 'A private tea party was held at the residence of Mr John Dean, of Silverwell House. There were at this party Messrs. Robert Heywood, Charles James Darbishire, Thomas Thomasson, James Winder, my brother Edmund and myself, with some others whose names I do not remember. The existing government of the Borough by Court Leet, under the authority of the Lord of the Manor, was discussed, and declared to be inappropriate and unworthy of the population, wealth and commercial character of the place. The result was that the little clique who met at John Dean's over a cup of tea advertised a public meeting, and prepared resolutions to be submitted thereat.'

The incorporators called a public meeting in Little Bolton Town Hall, and won all but unanimous support for their resolution in favour of a petition. The petition, signed by over 4000 persons, claimed that the inhabitants of Great and Little Bolton had no control over the officials placed in authority over them by the old manorial system, objected to the police having to be paid for out of the poor rates, and concluded by claiming that 'the obvious political bias which has prevailed in the selection of Boroughreeves and Constables for Great Bolton is not only unpopular and deprives the municipal officers of proper authority and assistance in their duties, but excludes from municipal office numbers of competent persons enjoying the confidence of their fellow townsmen. The population has been frequently acted upon by political excitement, involving riots and occasionally insecurity of life and property.'

The first attempt of the opponents of incorporation in Bolton misfired badly. Thomas Myerscough called a public meeting to oppose the petition largely on the grounds that Little Bolton, whose police charges were only one fifth of those of Great Bolton, and which was assessed at half the rateable value, would be victimized in any amalgamation. The incorporators turned up en masse and voted down the resolutions by a majority of twenty to one. But this feeling that Little Bolton should preserve its independence cropped up again from time to time.

There was, of course, a strong feeling, especially among Churchmen, of deference for the existing authorities, and a strong distrust of new, untried, and almost certainly more expensive forms of local government. The opponents of incorporation included most of the rich men of Bolton. They used their influence to get a counter-petition signed by over 3400 persons, which they claimed to be more than the number of ratepayers signing the original petition. This was the origin of the sharp cleft in Bolton local politics in the next four years. The counter-petitioners made the valid point that there was already some degree of popular participation in the affairs of both townships. There was not much merit in the assertion that the officials were chosen by representative juries in the Court Leet, because these juries were nominees of the Lords of the Manors. More to the point, in Great Bolton, 'the present Deputy Constable and two of the policemen now in office were appointed and their salaries fixed at a public meeting six years ago'. Recently, when a rate-payers' meeting rejected the Constables' accounts a poll was held which sustained both the system of appointment and the payment of salaries. As for Little Bolton 'the Trustees are appointed by the ratepayers and...have authority to appoint and pay policemen'. Neither side in the controversy mentioned the refusal of the Great Bolton Trustees to continue to allow public participation in the choice of new Trustees. The rule of this oligarchy behind closed doors roused Robert Heywood and many others to insist on municipal reform.

On February 24th 1839, Henry Ashworth, Robert Heywood, and James Winder the solicitor for the petitioners, presented the petition to the Privy Council, and as they were leaving they were confronted on the staircase by the deputation of their opponents, headed by William Bolling. Heywood was dismayed, but was reassured by Ashworth. Because of conflicting statements in the two petitions the Privy Council sent an investigator to Bolton, and he held an inquiry which lasted several weeks, mainly verifying signatures. No more was heard until October, and then a charter of incorporation arrived, addressed to James Winder, who thus almost automatically became the first Town Clerk. He arranged for the first election of Councillors in November.

The conservatives boycotted the election on the ground that the charter was invalid, and there were no contests. Robert Heywood became a Councillor for Church Ward. At the first meeting of the Town Council the thirty-six liberal Councillors chose twelve liberal Aldermen and made Charles Darbishire the first Mayor. Heywood was appointed to the Finance Committee and was one of ten magistrates appointed to sit on the bench in the Borough Court. He was the only borough magistrate in Bolton who was also a county magistrate.

It seemed as if the creation of the Corporation had merely added to the existing confusion of local affairs. Not only did all the rival authorities continue to act, but the Council, owing to defective legislation and the boycott, found itself almost entirely ineffective. It set up a Watch Committee which appointed a Police Superintendent, an inspector and ten policemen, dressed in blue uniforms, but the Deputy Constables and watchmen (the 'browns') still acted under the authority of the boroughreeve and Constables. Sometimes the two forces clashed, and brought charges of assault against each other in the rival courts. The first of the new police came mainly from Liverpool and were rather undisciplined. Once Heywood had to deal in court with charges of assault against the police and theft on the part of a police sergeant. He said: 'The magistrates will protect the police when they are proved to be within the path of duty. There is a bad feeling — I may call it a prejudice — against them, and it calls for great caution and gentleness on the part of the police. They are equally obliged to see that the privileges and liberties of the people are not infringed.'

Dual jurisdiction had its drawbacks. The Council appointed a Borough Coroner, but the County Coroner refused to give up his rights (until three years later when he was compensated for the loss) and two inquests were now held on each body, causing great inconvenience and sometimes producing different verdicts. When the new borough obtained the grant of a Court of Quarter Sessions and appointed a Recorder, he had difficulty in functioning because at first the Lancashire magistrates refused to allow the county jails to be used for the detention of prisoners committed from Bolton. The county magistrates of the Bolton division still judged cases from the borough at their Petty Sessions. During the Chartist alarms in 1839 Joseph Ridgway as spokesman for the irreconcilables applied to the Home Office for confirmation of their concurrent powers in Bolton, and when it was received this group of magistrates published a very provocative placard:

Borough of Bolton: Whereas a number of would-be gentlemen, presumptuously calling themselves Borough Magistrates, are in the habit of holding a Court over the Tap Room and Stables in Bowker's Row, and at such Court are granting summonses and Warrants, by those means obtaining funds to support their so-called Corporation: This is to give notice to the inhabitants of the Borough of Bolton that by applying at the said Court for Summonses and Warrants they are assisting the so-called Corporation to keep up the expensive farce of Mayor, Aldermen and Council-men. The inhabitants of the Borough are therefore requested to apply at the Old Police Office for all Summonses and Warrants as heretofore, it having been decided by the highest Legal Authority that the County Magistrates have jurisdiction within the borough.' (Quoted from F.C. Mather: *Public Order in the Age of the Chartists*, p.72).

Worst of all, it was impossible to finance the activities of the Corporation. Any rate levied had to be collected along with the poor rate, and the first move of the opponents of the charter was to secure the appointment, by a trick, of conservative Overseers of the Poor in Great Bolton instead of the radicals nominated by the ratepayers. This manoeuvre, the work of the local conservative county magistrates, was thwarted — as was a similar effort in Manchester — by a full meeting of magistrates at Salford Intermediate Sessions. Here there was a liberal majority, and four radical nominees were declared the rightful Overseers of Great Bolton for 1839. But they were soon in serious trouble. Conservative ratepayers, owning most of the largest properties in Bolton, refused to pay their rates. By May 1840 between £4000 and £5000 was owing, and the Guardians were threatening to distrain against the unfortunate Overseers to get their share of the arrears. The matter was only settled when the Town Clerk gave an undertaking not to claim any part of the money due for Corporation expenses. Corporation officials had to wait for payment of their salaries — fortunately they held part-time appointments. Members of the Town Council met legal charges and the cost of the police force from their own pockets.

Bolton Town Council had so little to do that it met only quarterly unless a special meeting was called. It had no control over the streets, which were the province of the Trustees and the Surveyor of Highways in each township, or over the markets, for which the Court Leet still appointed the officials. The Council, with little else to do, spent much of its time discussing resolutions on national affairs. Serious members wondered whether it was worth while having a charter at all. Robert Heywood was obviously disgusted by the impotence of the Council, and led the way in efforts to reach some compromise with opponents of the charter. The town was in the grip of the worst crisis it had ever had to face, and the cooperation of all its leaders was needed to cope with it. This was the Chartist outbreak of August 1839.

Until July 1839 the Bolton Chartists were relatively quiet. They held a number of meetings, and were allowed the use of Little Bolton Town Hall, where Bronterre O'Brien once spoke to them. More and more open talk of physical force alienated most of their middle class sympathizers, who had the same democratic aims but did not like the language of class war employed by the Chartists. In July Parliament rejected the petition for the People's Charter, which had been signed by over a million people. Chartists responded with demonstrations and riots, and proposed a general strike, called the 'sacred month' — later reduced to three days. Bolton became one of the main centres of trouble at this time. Charles Darbishire the Mayor remained reasonably friendly and unperturbed for as long as possible, and even allowed the Chartists to meet on 26th July in a field at The Folds belonging to his father, which they had been in the habit of using for open-air meetings. At this meeting they decided to demonstrate by attending the Parish Church for the morning service, and they marched there six abreast. Many were young boys, some of whom behaved boisterously in church, but in the end they listened to the sermon preached by the curate. A similar demonstration the next Sunday was thinly attended and passed off quietly. At their next open-air meeting, according to a report sent by the Mayor to the Home Office, some shots were fired.

On the next day, according to a diary compiled by Robert Heywood, 'the borough magistrates met to make arrangements for swearing in special constables', and Darbishire posted placards forbidding any more meetings in his father's field. On Monday 5th August 'notices were sent to the electors to attend on Wednesday and Thursday [for swearing in] subject to a penalty of £5. I also attended the Old Sessions Room,to inform the county magistrates of our proceedings, which appeared to be approved of.' Heywood was the link between the rival authorities that now began to cooperate to preserve order. 'Mr. Fletcher [John Fletcher, son of Colonel Ralph Fletcher and a county magistrate] stated that a pike had been observed by a lady who had nearly fainted in the church. Further inquiries were made but the parties did not like to appear to give evidence.' On Wednesday and Thursday 'the electors attend in great numbers to be sworn in'. 1500 special constables were enrolled. This calling up of a whole class of the community was most unusual. It may well have been a liberal plan to avoid depending too much on the regular soldiers. If so, it was almost completely ineffective.

Two companies of infantry were stationed permanently in overcrowded barracks in White Lion Brow, under the command of Lieutenant-colonel Cairncross. In peaceful times they were among the worst disturbers of the peace, through their drunkenness and readiness to attack civilians. In a crisis their discipline was excellent and their officers, under strict instructions from their liberal-minded commander Sir Charles Napier, acted only under orders from the magistrates, and then with the greatest restraint. (The other habitual disturbers of the peace in Bolton were the Irish of Newtown — the neighbourhood on either side of Great Moor Street. They had been told by their priests to have nothing to do with the Chartists, who were constantly attacking Daniel O'Connell and whose leader Feargus O'Connor was a protestant Irishman. On the whole they obeyed and abstained.)

On Monday, the first day of the strike, some of the mills shut down and the shops were closed for safety. George Lloyd spoke at several large meetings, and was supported by the other leaders Warden and Gillespie. The authorities kept a vigilant eye on the marches and assemblies of the Chartists, but there was little violence. The magistrates, however, decided that the leaders were inflammatory, and drew up warrants for their arrest.

The next morning — Tuesday 13th August — the Chartists met in the New Market Place at five o'clock. Before they dispersed the police arrived and arrested Lloyd, Warden and Gillespie. While they were being taken to Bowker's Row Police Office, a stone-throwing mob attacked the escort and rescued them. Lloyd and Warden were seized again and held in the Police Office, but Gillespie escaped. Heywood 'went to the town about half past six, found Lloyd and Warden apprehended, Gillespie escaped. Found the military assembled. A little after seven I accompanied the Mayor and Colonel Cairncross past the Dispensary into the square [Nelson Square] and to the Police Office. Engaged in the examinations of Lloyd and Warden. Commitment made out a little before twelve.'

The Chartist leaders put up a spirited defence. Warden said: 'If these magistrates do commit us, it will be for that which they themselves have advocated — for acting up to their example.' There was some exaggeration in this, but enough truth to delight the conservative opposition. They were committed to prison in Liverpool and could apply for bail to the Liverpool magistrates. (They soon obtained bail, and were freed at the next assizes on finding sureties for good behaviour.)

Before the police court proceedings the Mayor had been told that the mob had gone to Bolton Moor to intimidate workmen who had not turned out. He mounted the Town Clerk's horse and rode to the scene of the disturbance, where he spoke to the mob and urged them to be peaceful. They cheered him loudly, so loudly that his horse reared up and nearly threw him.

The arrest of their leaders greatly excited the crowds in the streets, and they were determined to rescue them once more. After the trial it was decided that the prisoners should be sent to Manchester by road with an escort of soldiers, and thence by train to Liverpool. Heywood reports: 'There was a delay of half an hour in consequence of the troops who were returning to Manchester not being ready; this caused a great crowd of people to be assembled, and on leaving the ground they were assaulted by stones etc.' The soldiers escorted the carriage with drawn swords. 'A large crowd followed them to the railway [Trinity Street Station] in expectation of rescuing them, and when they found them proceeding direct to Manchester they were exceedingly exasperated and returned furiously back into the town; on their way they assaulted Messrs. Kay and Holden [two solicitors] and when they arrived at the police they began throwing stones; a few windows were broken. One fellow I pursued down Back Mawdsley Street and Fold Street, crying out "Stop him"; but finding a stone thrown at me I was urged to enter the carrier's warehouse.' After dining at Silverwell House 'visited several parts of the town, found the people much exasperated, and the streets filling with people.'

The mob attacked two factories at this time to force the workpeople to turn out, and in one case soldiers dispersed the rioters. The bell of the Parish Church was tolled to call out the special constables. To resume the diary: 'About a quarter before four several respectable persons came up to me and represented .... that more vigorous measures should be taken to clear the streets. I had been of this opinion for some time and thought it would be advisable to take up some of the leaders. I went to the police office and appealed to the justices and they all consented ... Therefore in the absence of the Mayor I went up to Col. Cairncross and desired him to proceed in the best way to clear the streets. It was suggested that the Riot Act should be read.' The Act was read in four places, after which an hour must be allowed for it to be obeyed. 'During the hour I visited some groups and urged them to go home. A little after five I went to the Aspinwalls to see the streets cleared, took tea, found myself rather sickly and remained there nearly an hour and a half. The military did not manage so well.' By this time a troop of cavalry had arrived from Manchester. 'The cavalry went abreast and cleared the way pretty well, but the infantry marched by a large group in the Market Place and this increased their confidence. A large number of special constables also remained very inactive at the top of Bank Street. A great crowd was often to be seen in Bridge Street.'

'After leaving the Aspinwalls at seven I walked down Bradshawgate and then to the police. There met with Charles [the Mayor] and Mr. Lomax [a tory county magistrate] and walked away quietly with them to the barracks; must have arrived there at a quarter past seven, found the colonel at the mess... The conversation chiefly carried on between Mr. Lomax and the colonel as to the preparations for the night and the following day. The colonel said the men must have rest; they had been greatly harassed and could not turn out unless there was a riot.' After a visit to the railway station and a decision to send Lomax by train to Manchester for reinforcements Darbishire and Heywood 'came to the police — found the court crowded and several rioters undergoing an examination. Immediately on taking my seat a very urgent representation was made that the Town Hall [of Little Bolton] was in the possession of the rioters and would be burned down. C.D. (the Mayor) set off immediately.'

The most serious episode on this day of riots was the attack on Little Bolton Town Hall. A formidable mob had assembled there by six o'clock. The hall was protected by a body of special constables, one of whom ventured to arrest a ringleader, and as a result the mob attacked and drove 23 special constables to take refuge in the hall. They forced a lamp post out of the ground and with it battered down the main door, made their way upstairs after a fierce struggle, and drove the specials into a back room where they were able to hold out. They smashed most of the windows of the hall and demolished the furniture. For over two hours they remained in possession, until the Mayor alerted the troops and arrived with a contingent. One of the rioters is said to have fired a shot, harmlessly, whereupon the soldiers fired above the heads of the crowd, went in and dispersed them. The special constables were free. No one had been killed.

The next morning a special train carried the arrested rioters to Manchester. There were demonstrations on that day, the last of the strike, but they were fairly peaceful and the soldiers looked on quietly.   To the discipline and forbearance of the troops was mainly due the fact that not a single life had been lost during the riots.   The mayor and the magistrates had on the whole displayed firmness and good sense.   The *Bolton Chronicle* said that 'the magistrates were paralysed with fear', but this was contradicted by their strong opponent John Fletcher, who wrote a letter to the *Chronicle*: 'In common justice to the Mayor, I feel myself called upon to state, that as far as I was myself an eyewitness to his conduct, after uniting with him and the borough magistrates on the Tuesday afternoon, I did not observe any want of decision, or any lack of exertion to restore peace to the town.'

This tribute was the more remarkable because it was paid in the midst of a fierce controversy about the reasons for the long delay in rescuing the special constables at Little Bolton Town Hall.   When the first report of trouble reached the magistrates, the Mayor had sent Fletcher either to give a standby warning to the troops — as Fletcher maintained — or to ask Colonel Cairncross to send a body of soldiers to suppress the riot — as the Mayor claimed.   Incredibly neither the three magistrates nor the officer mentioned the subject when the magistrates called at the barracks while the riot was at its height — the territory across the Croal was still somewhat remote.   The different versions of what happened were never reconciled, though Lomax and Heywood drew up a statement and made considerable efforts to get both the Mayor and Fletcher to agree to its publication.   'No one can suppose that Mr. Fletcher would have hesitated in taking out the military had the order been clearly stated to him or that the other magistrates afterwards would have neglected such an important duty had they not fully believed the case had been provided for.   After all when due allowance has been made for the exasperated state of feeling of those unfortunate persons who were so long pent up in the Town Hall it cannot but be a source of the truest satisfaction to find the peace of the town was completely restored and that effected without the loss of a single life or even much damage to property.'

A garbled version of what had happened in Bolton was widely believed in London. When the Chartist riots were debated in the House of Lords, Lord Lyndhurst castigated the 'Chartist Mayor' and his colleagues, and the Duke of Wellington said: 'My Lords, we must put an end to the system of employing as magistrates for the preservation of peace the men who have been concerned in its violation.' The Mayor and the Town Clerk went to London and petitioned the House of Lords for an inquiry, but nothing was done.

These events drew attention to the need for adequate police forces in the new municipal boroughs, and Police Acts were speedily passed for all three, Birmingham, Manchester and Bolton, setting up forces modelled on the Metropolitan Police under Commissioners appointed by the Home Office, to be a charge on the local rates. The Bolton Police Act meant the end of the Constables and the 'brown' police in Bolton, and the transfer of the 'blues' to the new force. The Police Commissioner appointed in October 1839 resigned after a week, giving as his reason his refusal to command such a rabble. His successor was Sir Charles Shaw, Police Commissioner for Manchester, who for a year had charge of the Bolton force as well. The rate for this body was duly paid. Otherwise the Melbourne government, which might have been expected to come to the rescue of the new corporations with amending legislation, did nothing, while a long drawn out process in the High Court to test the validity of the Birmingham charter, kept them all in limbo. The Bolton Town Council drew back from independent legal action; the Councillors were afraid to risk having to pay the heavy charges themselves.

5. THE MAYORALTY AND THE HUNGRY FORTIES

When the time came to appoint a new Mayor for Bolton, the Councillors were no doubt influenced by the feeling that the only man who might bring the conservatives to accept the charter was Robert Heywood. All but one of the radicals supported his nomination, although the Chartist sympathizers now looked upon him as a backslider. In proposing him James Arrowsmith said he was 'of so much moderation he could scarcely be called a partisan'. The seconder said that he was highly respected by all parties. George Lloyd was present as a spectator, and as the Council was dispersing he interrupted and said he was 'quite surprised they had appointed a toryfied mayor; for he considered there was not a greater tory on the bench than Mr. Heywood'.

Heywood was absent from this meeting and at first refused office. He gave the extraordinary reason that he intended a prolonged visit to the continent; which shows how seriously he took these journeys for pleasure. One member of the Council 'understood that Mr. Heywood's appointment had been much approved of by the county magistrates, and he believed that one of them was at that moment with him, endeavouring to induce him to withdraw his objections'. Apparently he was persuaded that he might be a useful mediator, and agreed to take office.

At the first Council meeting after his appointment Robert Heywood clashed with Naisby and the radicals. Their aggressive attitude threatened to wreck the negotiations he had already started for a settlement with the opponents of the charter. In the end he persuaded Naisby to withdraw an inflammatory motion. He said: 'I was one of those who could make great allowances for the feelings of vexation and disappointment experienced by our opponents. Though they have acted upon the most exclusive and unjustifiable principles, I could not but think that we had also fallen in some degree into the same error.' He had to report failure so far to come to terms with the conservatives, and in fact in the end the negotiations broke down. Nevertheless the conservative *Chronicle* paid Heywood the only tribute to a political opponent to be found in its pages over many years. 'It is indeed a strange thing to find a gentleman of such fine sense, sound understanding, varied acquirements, and literary culture, in the political company of such dark, malicious good-for-nothings as he has to associate with. He might well call them to order and disapprove of their proceedings, but how can fine steel cut through blocks, or the points of gentlemanly reproof penetrate the hides of such vulgar beings.' It is the language of Eatanswill.

Three South Wales Chartists, Frost, Williams and Jones, had been condemned to death for their leadership of the Chartist rising in Newport, and the Bolton Chartists proposed an open-air meeting in February to petition the Queen for a pardon. Because there were still troops in the town the Chartist leaders waited on the borough magistrates to ask for protection. Heywood wanted to be sure that the meeting would confine itself to the subject-matter of the memorial. 'I give no sanction to the meeting, remember; on the contrary I am opposed to it because it is unwise and unpolitic.'   Eventually the Chartists held their meeting in a public house.   Much to Heywood's annoyance the Council voted by fifteen votes to twelve in favour of a memorial on behalf of the condemned Chartists.   He so strongly disapproved that he said that if he could do so with propriety he would decline to sign it on behalf of the Council.   'I do not sit here to be dictated to.'

The Council drew up an address congratulating Queen Victoria on her marriage. This was no mere formality, for the young Queen had been very popular with the liberals ever since the 'bedchamber crisis' of 1839, when she had prevented Sir Robert Peel from forming a government and restored to office the whig Lord Melbourne.   In 1839 the liberals, with the Mayor in the chair, had held their own dinner in the Commercial Inn, to rival the more flamboyantly patriotic dinner of the Boroughreeve and the conservatives at the Swan.   Now Robert Heywood, as Mayor, presented the address from the Council at a royal levée.   Peter Ainsworth, the Bolton M.P., wrote to him about this visit, explaining the procedure, and added: 'If you are ambitious of the honour of knighthood, you will please to inform me and I will make it known in the proper quarter.'   Heywood refused to be considered.   Other mayors attending in the same way were knighted.

All other problems during Robert Heywood's mayoralty were dwarfed by that of distress and misery due to the worst depression Bolton had ever had to face. Trade had never really recovered after the slump of 1837, and in the latter part of 1839 was rapidly worsening.   Failures were common and suicides not unknown. Dr. Bythell *(The Handloom Weavers)* gives as an example of a kindly firm of manufacturers R. & J. Mangnall, who gave a dinner for their weavers to celebrate the coronation of Queen Victoria.   Heywood wrote to William Bowker in New Jersey in February 1840: 'You will be very sorry to hear of the melancholy death of poor James Mangnall.   It appears they had not been so successful in business as was generally supposed and a good deal of blame has been laid on Mrs. Ralph's expensive habits.   About six months ago James found it necessary to call his creditors together and though an arrangement was soon made to take 12/- or 15/- in the pound it proved too much for poor James to bear, his mind became seriously affected and early one morning about six weeks ago he was found in the agonies of death, having cut his throat in the most dreadful manner ... Trade... very depressed... handloom weaving extremely low — most of the cotton mills working short time and two or three in this neighbourhood entirely closed.   Garnett Taylor of Astley Bridge has again suspended payment throwing out of employment more than 1000 hands.   Many of our large foundries and machine shops have not half work.   All these circumstances together with the high price of provisions have created great and general distress.'   Wages in the mills were reduced by 8—10%, and a strike against this reduction broke down.   It was said that 1600 houses in the town were empty.   Many families had pawned all their furniture, and had only rags for bedding and clothing.   In a parliamentary debate it was assumed that Bolton was the most distressed town in England, although the local M.P.'s thought that conditions were as bad in some other industrial towns.

The relief of this appalling mass of poverty was in the first place the responsibility under the new Poor Law of the Board of Guardians of the Bolton Union, a body elected by the ratepayer with county magistrates as ex-officio members, and supervised by the Poor Law Commission, who stationed an Assistant Commissioner in Manchester to keep a close watch on the industrial towns. There was no question in industrial Lancashire of applying the workhouse test for relief. The Guardians gave outdoor relief, and even supplemented the earnings of the lowest paid wage earners with families by making allowances for children.

From the inception of the Board in 1837 Great and Little Bolton returned radicals or liberals as Guardians, but they were always outvoted by a large mass of reactionary Guardians representing the 24 rural townships in the Union. In these the landowners still had a firm control, and there were hardly ever any elections. The majority of the Guardians bitterly resented any interference from the Commissioners, and were ruthless in their determination to keep down the poor rate. Robert Shaw of Lostock was the extreme example; he was a local Pooh Bah, Constable, Overseer and Surveyor of Highways as well as Guardian for Lostock. He spoke in a broad dialect carefully reproduced in the local press. Once he said that the best way to get rid of vermin in the workhouse would be to boil the pauper inmates. On one occasion he forgot to go through the formalities of his re-election, and was most indignant when he was temporarily excluded from the Board. The Assistant Commissioner was constantly concerned with the irregularities of his administration; once, in exasperation, he burst out: 'Mr Shaw did not care much about the law, but he might find the law would be too strong for him in a little time.'

There was constant bickering and much personal abuse at the meetings of the Board of Guardians. Magistrates attended infrequently — some not at all; Robert Heywood, the one most often present, obviously found his position distasteful and could achieve little. He was the custodian of the interests of the Great Bolton Trust, which owned the workhouse, and of the Dispensary, which received pauper patients; once during a heated dispute over payments of 3/- a week for these he protested against 'gross personal abuse'.

At the meeting of the Town Council in February 1840 Heywood spoke strongly about the inadequacy of the allowances paid by the Guardians. A leader in the *Bolton Free Press* alleged that they were sometimes as low as eightpence a week, and the average allowance was said to be 1/3, less than the amount, 1/6½ a week, given some time previously by Heywood as the cost of food per head in the workhouse. He proposed to ask the Trustees of Great and Little Bolton for joint action, and had already secured the promise of Rev. James Slade, the Vicar of Bolton, to cooperate. The Council authorized him to meet the Boroughreeves, and as a result a meeting backed by all these authorities, with the Vicar in the chair, considered the state of the distressed poor. A resolution was carried urging the Guardians to be more generous; but, except in extreme emergency, they could relieve only those people who had a settlement in Bolton. The meeting decided that a Fund for the Relief of the Poor should be instituted, to help long-term residents who could get no relief from the Guardians because they had no settlement. Robert Heywood was appointed secretary of the committee and headed the subscription list.

The thrifty and businesslike management of the fund anticipated the methods of the Charity Organization Society. It made use of inspectors to prevent fraud, and issued periodical public statements of the number of cases investigated, number relieved, number rejected and grounds of rejection. All in receipt of relief were offered free whitewash to cleanse their dwellings, and where there was no able bodied person the labour to apply it. Eventually a permanent body emerged, the Poor Protection Society, which functioned in Bolton for many years to supplement the ordinary poor relief. Heywood ceased to be secretary, but remained on the committee.

By such means thousands of people were kept barely alive. There was no catastrophic rise in the death rate (already one of the highest in England) nor widespread emigration, as in Ireland after 1846. The extreme misery is illustrated by a number of letters from handloom weavers in the *Free Press*. One who did 'journeywork' said that his net income was 3/- a week, out of which he had to pay 1/- as rent, 10d. for coals, and 3d. for candles. He was married and had two children, and his wife also had two children by a previous marriage for whom they received 2/- allowance. They lived in a damp cellar, and had a bedstead, a scanty bed with an old sheet and cover, but no other furniture whatever. The wife had no chemise to wear, neither had the three girls, but the boy had a shirt. They were 'shivered to death'. Their only food was water gruel twice a day.

The town was so poor at this time that the Great Bolton Trustees decided that they could not levy a rate. Heywood proposed that they should cancel all expenditure on the maintenance of the fire equipment and give up the street lights in Great Bolton. Dark nights and increased dangers added to the misery of the town.

No wonder that Robert Heywood was despondent about the futility of the Council in face of these problems. In August 1840 there was no business to discuss except the payment of a few bills amounting to £130. His mayoralty ended in gloom, made worse by a serious illness. A wound in the leg, caused when he fell on a flowerpot in the garden, became poisoned and confined him to his house for two months, and he recovered just in time to preside over the meeting which elected his successor, James Arrowsmith.

The depression of 1840-2 gave great force to the campaign of the Anti-Corn Law League. Cheaper bread would save lives and alleviate distress. Cobden was the political Messiah of the hungry forties, though rejected by most Chartists. The Bolton opponents of the Corn Law invited Cobden to be their candidate in the general election of 1841, but he preferred Stockport, where he had stood previously. Bolton reformers then secured Dr. John Bowring, the first man to have spoken in favour of the repeal of the Corn Law at a Manchester meeting, and a powerful advocate. Heywood took the chair at two huge meetings during the campaign, at the second of which Cobden made a stirring speech. Bowring held large and noisy meetings of non-electors, with the Chartist sympathizer Isaac Barrow in the chair, and convinced the majority of his audiences that he was their sincere friend. The other candidates were Ainsworth, lukewarm over the Corn Law question, and the conservatives Bolling and Peter Rothwell, a partner in the oldest engineering firm, one of the leading Methodists, and a philanthropist whose soup kitchen kept many starving people alive during the depression. Both the conservatives declared themselves in favour of a reduction in the corn duty. But this was not enough. Bolton broke its rule of returning one member of each party and returned Ainsworth at the head of the poll and Bowring second. Bolling, the sitting member, came last. It was a rowdy and probably a dirty election. Rothwell said he had been beaten by bribery and intimidation.

Heywood continued to work for free trade in corn. He did as the League advised by buying up several freeholds in different constituencies to multiply his voting power. He assiduously attended the tea parties, dinners and banquets in Bolton and Manchester which played an important part in the well organized campaign, and where he often proposed the 'sentiments' which replaced toasts at these teetotal gatherings. He took the chair at a meeting of women in December 1841, which resulted in a petition for repeal signed by 16,000 Bolton women. He later subscribed modest sums – 50 guineas in 1844, £100 in 1845, to the cause. But there were in Bolton rich millowners who subscribed less than Heywood did to charities, but gave as much as £1000 to the League. Obviously Heywood did not regard the repeal of the Corn Laws as a panacea as did some of his friends.

When the victory was won by Peel's action in repealing the Corn Laws in June 1846, Heywood subscribed £50 to Cobden's testimonial and £5 to Bright's, though he thought there ought to have been 'one general fund to be distributed proportionally among the various individuals who have taken an active part in promoting and successfully carrying the great measure so important to the welfare of the country'. At that time he was so much moved by the starvation in Ireland and the shortage of food in Britain because of the failure of the potato crop that he took the lead in Bolton in demanding the immediate opening of the ports, as an emergency measure before the Act could take effect, to the free import of corn.

During this period many reformers lost sight of other political issues in their fanatical enthusiasm for repeal. Robert Heywood did not. He was active in a nonconformist campaign against an Education Bill which would grant aid to Church schools, and spoke in favour of purely secular education. He believed in more leisure for the working class, and was a strong supporter of Ashley's campaign for the Ten Hours Bill. He went to London to give evidence in favour of this measure before the parliamentary committee on the Bill, which became law in 1847. (Dr. Bowring voted against it.) But local problems and issues were still his prime concern and although the Corporation was a disappointment – he lost his seat on the Council in 1844 – he had abundant scope for his energies, as magistrate, Trustee, Guardian and private philanthropist.

Before prosperity began to return there was one more serious threat to public order in Lancashire, the Plug Riots of 1842. By that time the Chartists in Bolton were rather subdued. Their meetings, held indoors usually in their own headquarters, were modestly attended even when Feargus O'Connor paid them a visit. The *Bolton Free Press* insisted that the new outbreak of violence was the result of poverty not of Chartism, but the local Chartists became active in instigating trouble. [For a full account see *The Plug Riots of 1842 in Lancashire and Cheshire,* by A. G. Rose, in the *Transactions of the Lancashire and Cheshire Antiquarian Society Vol. XVII – 1957.*]

To begin with it was a confused and largely spontaneous mass movement of the infuriated poor, begging for food and money with menaces. Many unemployed and handloom weavers joined the mill workers in massive demonstrations, which took the form of forcing mills and factories still working to shut down by drawing the plugs of the engine boilers. Mobs of demonstrators marched from town to town; they were bolder away from home.

Ashton-under-Lyne was the first Lancashire centre, and when the Ashton men aroused Manchester the rioting spread rapidly throughout industrial Lancashire. On 10th August, the day after the worst riot in Manchester, an Ashton leader urged the Bolton workers to strike with the threat that the Ashton men would come and give them a 'good walloping' unless they did. During the next two days a few mills were shut down by force, and on 12th August the police were stoned and the Riot Act read.

On Saturday 13th August 1842, the third anniversary of the previous big riot, a crowd of 5000 invaded Bolton from Bury, levying contributions from shopkeepers and publicans. The magistrates called out troops and armed the police, but no action was taken as the mob drew the plugs at Bolling's mill and the engineers Benjamin Hick and Son were stopped from working. One or two other mills were attacked. The rioters brandished bludgeons and iron bars. The Riot Act was again read, but there were no major clashes, and when the mob returned to Bury all was quiet. The magistrates were so little alarmed that the next morning they discharged the rioters taken prisoner on their entering into recognizances to keep the peace. As a precaution they swore in a number of special constables.

On Monday a local demonstration was organized. The demonstrators assembled early; there were some speeches and at one meeting they passed resolutions in favour of the People's Charter and the Ten Hours Bill. Finally, they made up their minds to march to Wigan to draw the plugs there, and between two and three thousand set off. At Chequerbent they put a stop to the Bolton and Leigh Railway by drawing the plug in the stationary engine which drew trains up the incline from Bolton. Reinforcements of troops arrived in Bolton from Manchester. One party of invaders from Bury was diverted into the outlying districts, but a large and violent crowd from Farnworth entered the town by the Manchester Road. Robert Heywood was one of the county magistrates who decided to go with the soldiers and police to confront this mob. The magistrates were Heywood and Darbishire, both on foot, and Lomax, Hulton, Ridgway and Barnes, all on horseback. They took up their positions in front of a body of infantry and yeomanry cavalry in Bradshawgate. (The contrast with Peterloo should be noticed.) The rioters pressed up to the magistrates brandishing cudgels, but the loaded muskets intimidated them and they fell back, dispersing into the side streets. The yeomanry galloped after the runaways, who fell over one another and some of whom fell into the canal. No one was killed or seriously injured.

This show of force stirred up some excited hostility in Bolton and three times the yeomanry dispersed a mob in Bradshawgate. They restrained themselves well, but the Peterloo reputation clung to them and their use by the authorities was always provocative. On this occasion only one man is recorded as having been struck by a sword and cut on the nose; his attacker was said to have been John Fletcher, the magistrate, a lieutenant in the yeomanry, whose father, Ralph Fletcher, had rushed into the crowd at Peterloo hitting people with his stick.

After this hectic day the riots subsided. Within ten days all the workers were back at work. Trade was beginning to improve, and Bolton's next great public excitement was a demonstration of industrial achievement. In September 1842 the highest chimney in England — 360 feet high — belonging to William Blinkhorn's chemical works, was completed, to the discharge of cannon, the ascent of a balloon out of the chimney, and a firework display from its top. According to the *Free Press:* 'Bombshells will be thrown upwards of 1000 feet from the top... Mr Fisher's excellent cornucopean band will ascend to the top of the chimney and play there'. During the next week thousands of people ascended the chimney to get a bird's eye view of their town with its forest of chimneys. Prospects began to brighten, except for the remaining handloom weavers.

In this cruel time one of the blackest spots in Bolton was its workhouse. The extreme economizers on the Board of Guardians were also the strongest opponents of workhouses and of central direction, and they not only refused to build the new workhouse which the Poor Law Commissioners wanted, but for a long time refused to improve the existing overcrowded workhouse, a group of converted cottages. The more enlightened conservative county magistrates, such as Rev. J.S. Birley of All Saints Church and W.F. Hulton, were very critical of the Guardians, and worked with Robert Heywood and Charles Darbishire for improvements, against a stubborn reactionary majority.

The Poor Law Commissioners kept up a constant presssure. In October 1842 they investigated the case of an old woman found to have died of starvation, and sent a letter to the Guardians asking for a more careful scrutiny of the poor. Almost immediately afterwards the scandalous condition of the workhouse roused them to action. In December James Flitcroft, a prominent local radical, went to the Guardians' meeting, and created a disturbance by producing a little box containing, so he said, five hundred fleas taken from the body of his brother Thomas, one of forty pauper lunatics in the workhouse. It was at this time that Robert Shaw made his famous remark about boiling the paupers. Whilst this was causing excitement in and about the workhouse, a drunken nurse there, becoming impatient because an old woman she was nursing took so long to die, insisted that she was dead before she was, and had her laid out and removed to the mortuary, where she was seen to move her arm.

Several workhouse inmates defied authority by attending the county magistrates' court the next day and demanding an investigation. The publicity they secured in this way roused into action the Assistant Poor Law Commissioner in Manchester, Hon. C.S. Clements, who found such a state of negligence that he insisted on the dismissal of the Master and Mistress of the workhouse, and the resignation of the Medical Officer. He drew up a scathing report. 'It is impossible to read the evidence given by the Master, without feeling that a state of things more incompatible with order, industry, good morals, health or common decency, cannot be imagined to exist. Able men and their wives, young women, children of all ages, mingled together in the same sleeping room and the same yard. The aged and the young, covered with vermin; infants, patients suffering from scarlet fever or scald heat, and children free from disease, all cooped up in the confined rooms of a series of cottages... This is such a communication as we have rarely or never had to address to any board.'

At the next meeting of the Guardians the magistrates turned up in greater force than usual, and Birley and Heywood carried a resolution that a committee should be appointed with a competent surveyor to consider alterations to the workhouse. They, Hulton and four elected Guardians constituted the committee. There were some scenes at this meeting. Heywood was 'insulted in a most ungentlemanly manner', and hoped that the reporters would not detail the disgraceful squabbles which took place at the meetings of the Board. The committee's recommended improvements, the cost of which was estimated at £10,000, were rejected by the full Board, and only minor alterations were agreed upon.

Meanwhile, Flitcroft had made use of the right of public access to the Guardians' accounts, and discovered that pigs kept at the workhouse and fed by its swill had been killed to supply pork and bacon to some of the Guardians, including John Bolling, the chairman. Heywood insisted that this abuse must be stopped, and Darbishire tried unsuccessfully to get a hearing for Flitcroft at the Board. At one point the chairman referred to 'Mr Darbishire and his lousy colleague Flitcroft'. It is easy to see why liberal magistrates were reluctant to attend such disorderly proceedings.

Heywood's persistence in his efforts to improve the workhouse at last produced some results. In 1845 a major renovation was carried out. Four W.C's were installed, and even steam central heating, and soon afterwards bathrooms. If he is to be believed, the food at the workhouse was better than the accommodation. He once asserted that the food was 'good enough for any person'. On New Year's Day at least, the inmates were well fed; the chairman presided over a dinner of roast beef and plum pudding.

One of Robert Heywood's main concerns at this time was the supply of water to the town. He had learned much about reservoirs by taking the lead, along with the bleacher James Hardcastle, in constructing Entwistle Reservoir in 1831, on land which was part of an estate owned by his father. This was a public utility administered by a trust under an Act of Parliament, regulating the industrial water supply of Bradshaw Brook, and charging tolls to the users. It was rather an unprofitable concern; he lent it £10,000, and the interest was always in arrears until the Corporation relieved him of the burden in 1866 by buying the reservoir. Enlarged, it is now the town's largest single source of drinking water.

Bolton-le-Moors was well placed for obtaining a pure supply of water from its hinterland (which still supplies the town with most of its requirements). As early as 1823 the Bolton Waterworks Company was formed, and constructed Belmont Reservoir. Heywood was very critical of this body. He thought it made an excessive profit; and its charges prevented many of the working class from having a supply. There were no standpipes in the streets for general use, and poor people were sometimes summoned and fined heavily for stealing water by taking it from a neighbour's supply.

Heywood thought that a free municipal supply of water was essential to the health of the town. He tried to get the Great Bolton Trust to act, but too many of the Trustees had a financial interest in the existing waterworks. At last he saw an opportunity for action in 1842, when the Manufacturing Districts Relief Fund offered a grant to provide employment for the poor. All told, £2600 was received from this source, and administered by the Poor Protection Society. Heywood proposed the construction of a reservoir on Bolton Moor, handy for the worst slums in Bolton, but a site where the danger of contamination was considerable — this was not very well understood at the time. The plan was accepted and 300 men were employed. When the fund was used up he persuaded the Trust to assume responsibility and complete the work. It was the only project for the relief of the heavy unemployment in Bolton at that time. When the reservoir was completed the Trustees set up 27 standpipes in the poorest part of Bolton for the free supply of the people.

As soon as the new water supply was secured, Robert Heywood turned his attention to the erection of public baths, a project which he had had in mind since he had taken the chair at a public meeting on the subject in 1841. Serious operations began in July 1844. The Earl of Bradford gave a site in Bridgeman Street, and the Waterworks Company offered a free supply of water; £5 shares were issued, and within a month nearly £2000 was subscribed. Heywood was a major subscriber and a member of the committee of management. James Greenhalgh, the architect, drew up plans which show that the baths were not intended solely for the benefit of the poor. 'Behind the ladies' waiting room will be tepid, warm and cold baths; adjoining them, but separated by a partition, will be baths of a common kind for females of the lower ranks. Behind the gentlemen's room are their tepid, warm and cold baths, and beyond that the large plunge bath, for workmen and others, which will be 48 feet by 20 feet.'

The project was delayed by party squabbling. The radical Greenhalgh was dismissed, Whittaker, a rival architect, appointed, and the Vicar of Bolton took the chair. But by July 1845 the chairmanship was in the hands of the liberal bleacher J.H. Ainsworth, Greenhalgh was restored as architect, and the capital was increased to £3500. The *Chronicle* alleged that the delays were due to 'parties who do not possess any great share of public esteem' taking the lead, but an indignant letter-writer in the *Free Press,* clearly referring to Heywood, said that 'if the editor had as sincere a desire for the welfare of the town as that gentleman (overlooking certain peculiarities) he would display a much different spirit. Although differing diametrically from that gentleman in politics, I do say that a meed of praise is due to him for the active part he is taking not only in the baths, but in the reservoir on Bolton Moor.'

In 1846 the committee decided to build an assembly room over the baths, and soon Heywood was helping to organize a series of 'Gentlemen's Concerts' for subscribers. In August the working men's bath was opened; the admission charge was 1½d. The baths are still in use.

In 1846 Samuel Kent of the Life and Health Association of Liverpool gave two lectures in Bolton on public health. Robert Heywood was chairman at the first lecture, and contrary to his usual practice spoke from the chair on a subject which moved him more than any other. He said more should be done for 'the improvement of the working classes... No person could walk through the streets of Bolton and witness some of the confined and miserable dwellings of the poor — cellars dark and ill-ventilated, without being convinced that something ought to be done to remedy the evil... It is in a very favourable position for drainage. We have an abundant supply of water, which is likely to be still further increased. Public baths are also in course of erection... I shall not be satisfied until we have washhouses also, that the poor may have their clothes washed with less inconvenience... Neither shall I be satisfied till plots of land shall have been purchased in two or three parts of the town... to be appropriated as playgrounds and places of public recreation.'

The lecturer attacked bad housing. He said Liverpool was the most unhealthy town in England, with an average age at death of 17, but Bolton was next worst, with an average age of 19. Birmingham was the most healthy town in England because it was the least crowded. He had visited a cellar dwelling in Bow Street which was 'like going down into a well...the effluence as he entered the door was enough to cause death and disease to the whole town'. In 1848 cholera and typhus caused many deaths in the town owing to these housing conditions, but children's infectious diseases were in the long run the worst pest of all.

6. THE TRIUMPH OF THE CORPORATION

Because of his intense concern about public health and welfare, Robert Heywood was the strongest and most consistent advocate in Bolton of municipalization of services. He wanted a strong Corporation with extensive power to act. Paradoxically this was achieved by his opponents, who entered the Council in 1842, gained control in 1844, and liquidated the Trusts in 1850.

The Great and Little Bolton Trusts, dominated respectively by conservatives and liberals, continued to play a big part in local government in the 1840s, dealing with roads, the coming of the railways, street trading and the market, fire protection, sanitation, and the lighting of the town. Their resources were far too small for their tasks. Extreme economy was forced on the Great Bolton Trust, by the attitude of the ratepayers who unreasonably expected the Trust to perform all these tasks out of its income from the Moor rents, and resented the levying of the so-called police rate in addition to the poor rate and the borough rate – a heavy burden in bad times. Stern economies such as the abandonment of street lighting balanced the accounts, and in 1842 Heywood reported a bank debt of only £102. The lighting of the streets was resumed, but only during 'the dark of the moon'.

Robert Heywood was not to remain treasurer of the Great Bolton Trust for much longer. In 1843 he proposed and the Town Council decided on an application to Parliament for leave to bring in a bill to take over the Trusts and to establish a municipal waterworks. The trustees decided that he had betrayed his trust and was no longer fit to hold the treasurership; he had only two supporters in a small meeting. But by May 1844 he was able to say in a Town Council meeting that the Trustees were becoming more favourable to the Corporation, and that there was now a considerable feeling in favour of amalgamation. This was an outcome of the entry of conservatives into the Council.

In 1842 Peel's government carried a bill that firmly established the new corporations, with the restoration of their control of the police. The conservatives in Bolton contested the municipal elections in November 1842. They had always had a strong following in Bolton, especially among Churchmen, and now won nine of the thirteen contested seats. Their victory was partly due to a demand they had made for the further reduction of the inadequate police force, which the Council had already reduced from 40 men to 20. The next year some of the leading liberals of Little Bolton discredited their party by an unsuccessful attempt to disfranchise by a trick all the conservative voters there. This rebounded on them, and the conservatives gained eight seats. The next year completed the rout of the liberals. Heywood, who had refused to canvass or to hold meetings, polled only 72 votes in Church Ward, where his leading opponent had 220. The conservatives won seven seats and were able to elect six aldermen, and there were now 29 conservatives and 19 liberals on the Council. They dismissed the Town Clerk, James Winder, and appointed in his place J.K. Watkins, their own henchman.

At this election Robert Heywood issued an election address in the form of a poster: 'If you should think proper to re-elect me, I will again endeavour to do my duty: but to obtain such honour I shall not have recourse to canvassing, nor will I request any individual to perform such degrading service for me. I further declare, that I will not spend one penny in aid of the vicious system of treating, or any other illegal act so truly debasing to the community; but, on the contrary, with the view of putting down such abominations as far as possible, I hereby offer the sum of Fifty Pounds to be paid on the conviction of any person so offending in this or any other of the respective wards.' (There is a footnote quoting the clause in the Corporation Act dealing with corrupt practices.)

'I also cannot but express my regret at witnessing so much political party feeling manifested on these occasions; for though, perhaps, unavoidable in some degree in a Parliamentary contest, it has always appeared to me uncalled for in the election of municipal officers, whose duty should be to see that the borough remain well and quietly governed, which I think, and have often declared, can only be effected in a satisfactory manner by all parties being duly represented.'

The swing against the liberals became even stronger in succeeding years, and for three years there were only six liberals in the Council. Heywood himself was not re-elected until 1851, although he made an attempt to return in 1846. By that time the conservatives had revived the project of taking over the Trusts and intended to buy the waterworks, and Heywood had become the spokesman of the Great Bolton Trust and was working closely with Burton, a conservative Little Bolton Trustee, on these plans for a takeover. He and Burton were nominated for the two seats in East Ward, and hoped to avoid a contest. But radicals denounced this pact, put up two candidates at the last moment, and won the election. Heywood wrote a letter to the electors, in which he said that he was not much disappointed, as 'anything approaching a coalition is apt to be viewed unfavourably by both parties, more especially by beersellers and others of guzzling propensities.'

When the liberals were defeated, some of them tried to organize a rival waterworks company. Heywood, who had employed a surveyor to explore the possibilities, thought that enough water could be obtained from Heaton to supply Bolton and Salford as well. (He had originally proposed a reservoir at Rivington, some years before Liverpool took up this project.) At this time water schemes proliferated. A third plan for Bolton, which came to nothing, was to run a conduit from the moors above Darwen underneath the tracks of the new Blackburn railway. Heywood soon withdrew from the Heaton project, but its other promoters persisted, and it looked for a time as if Bolton might have two waterworks companies (Sheffield had two gas companies). In the end the Bolton Waterworks Company made a handsome offer to take over the project, it was accepted, and the company applied to Parliament for a new bill to give powers to build reservoirs in Heaton and Rumworth to augment its supplies. This roused the public authorities to action. In 1846 Heywood, representing the Great Bolton Trust, sat on a committee with members of the Town Council; they pressed for reduction of charges and the limitation of profits to 10%. He went to London to promote these aims when the Bill was before a committee of the House, and had the satisfaction of seeing the amendments he wanted put into the Act.

By this time a group of progressive conservatives was coming to the fore in the Council. They believed in the Corporation and municipal enterprise, and promoted the Bolton Improvement Act of 1846, which gave the Corporation power to buy the waterworks and take over the Trusts. By 1850 this programme was completed. Now that the prospect of high profits had vanished, the Waterworks Company soon came to terms with the Corporation. The Great Bolton Trust handed over its powers in 1849 — its assets, apart from the Bolton Moor rents, included lamps and lamp pillars £797, four fire engines, hose etc. £325, land and buildings £2500, and Bolton Moor waterworks £5555. The Little Bolton Trust had a liberal majority at this time, and led by Thomas Thomasson put up a short separatist rearguard action, but this collapsed when the Corporation threatened parliamentary measures.

The Corporation was now an effective body. In 1848 it had acquired new sanitary powers under the Public Health Act of that year, and with the warning of the typhus and cholera epidemics (for which fever sheds had had to be built) freshly in mind, set about the task of cleaning up the town. The conservatives constructed new reservoirs at Heaton and Rumworth. In 1852 they set up a public library which eventually took over the Exchange News Room and Library to which Heywood had contributed so much. T.L. Rushton, the most important municipal leader in this period, had daring plans for reconstruction in the town centre. He pushed through the project of a covered Market Hall, a superb example of engineer's iron and glass work with porticoed entrances, one of the finest in England. Some of the worst slums in Bolton were demolished to make room for this and for adjoining shopping streets, Market Street, Corporation Street, and the broad Knowsley Street crossing the Croal at a high level.

This imaginative town-planning, the greatest justification of the Corporation's existence, was opposed as a piece of grandiose extravagance by the economical Robert Heywood and the liberals. Some jobbery was discovered, and the voters turned heavily against the conservatives. By 1853 the liberals had won back a majority which they kept for the rest of Heywood's lifetime; in fact for two years after that the conservatives did not even contest the elections. Heywood, elected Councillor in 1851, was made an Alderman in 1854, and held this position until his death.

7. LONELINESS AND MARRIAGE

While Robert Heywood was so actively engaged in public affairs in the 1830's and 1840's, his private life was a lonely one. His diary for 27th May 1832 reads 'I lost the greatest friend on earth this forenoon'. His father had been ailing and increasingly helpless for some years, yet this man of 45 was morbidly afflicted by the final separation. For months afterwards he recorded dreams of his father. 'Dreamed about interring my dear father from the old house and letting him slip into Baxter's yard; obliged to take him back in a decayed state till the following morning.' 'Dreamed that my father was raised from the dead.' 'Dreamed a good deal as usual about my father, he appeared, shook hands with me and patted my face to console me. Nearly a year later he still 'dreamed almost every night during the last week of my late dear father'. In September 1833: 'First day without weeping for my poor father, but I have not yet forgot him!'

Heywood visited America in 1834, an invigorating journey which helped him to recover from his melancholy. The outward voyage in the 'Britannia' was a very stormy one and took six weeks. As there were only nine cabin passengers on board each had a double berth to himself. Heywood made friends with two parsons, and once shared two bottles of champagne with them at a dinner — in England he was a teetotaller. In the crowded steerage, with its 140 passengers, measles broke out among the children, and four were buried at sea.

Robert Heywood's primary purpose in visiting the United States was to see his numerous friends and acquaintances from Bolton who had settled there. He met a number in New York; he then went by steamboat along the New Jersey coast landed and made his way inland to a farm near Princeton, where he stayed with William Bowker, son of the Unitarian Boroughreeve of Peterloo year, who lived in 'a beautiful white cottage....Walked round the farm, about fifty acres which cost him 7 guineas an acre. The soil good and well cultivated with rye, oats, maize... The estate is beautifully varied by gentle elevations; never troubled by mosquitoes most of the snakes have been destroyed. They have five horses, seven cows, thirty pigs, two hundred poultry, besides pigeons etc... Very careful, exceedingly diligent rising at four and working till eight, doing all the carpenter's work, butchering, etc. From this friend Heywood on his return had for some years annual gifts of barrels of Newtown Pippins.

When he reached Philadelphia Heywood found that a drunken uncle of his, whom he had hoped to meet, had cut his throat three weeks before. He admired the industries of Philadelphia and attended the theatre, and from there went to Washington by steamboat. He visited the House and the Senate, and had a talk with Henry Clay the most eminent senator of his time. He was taken to the White House and introduced to President Andrew Jackson.

From the capital Heywood set out on a long, rough journey through the mountains by very bad roads, and down the Ohio valley, in part by steamboat, as far as

Lexington, Kentucky, to look up old friends. Then he doubled back to Pittsburg, whose smoke made him homesick, and thence to see the wonders of Niagara Falls, including the walk under the fall from Goat Island. Lake steamers took him by way of Toronto to Montreal — 'a small, uninteresting place' — and to Quebec, still visiting friends. After that he travelled, again mainly by steamboat, to Albany on the Hudson, and thence to Boston. Here one of his main objects was to see and hear Dr Channing, the high priest of Unitarianism, but Channing was away at Newport, Rhode Island, for the summer; thither Heywood went, but only just in time to see him leaving for a journey and to shake his hand.

He now returned to New York and made another journey into the Catskill Mountains to see an old aunt Alice Makinson from Little Lever. He found her and her husband comfortably settled on a 160 acre farm on the slopes, where they made their own sugar from maple syrup and their own soap from wood ashes. Their children lived at home or near by, and he found 'all the neighbours sociable and kind... Nothing like stealing is known, all the houses without lock or bolt.' From this pleasant spot he travelled roughly to Northumberland, Pennsylvania, where his Bolton friends introduced him to a grandson of Joseph Priestley, and he paid his respects at Priestley's grave and at the house where he had died, and saw 'a beautiful willow planted by the doctor'. Somewhat later in the tour he made another pilgrimage to Poughkeepsie, to the grave of John Taylor, the Bolton radical.

Heywood spent three months in America. He had suffered much discomfort from the heat, the mosquitoes, and the primitive accommodation in many small towns where beds for travellers were scarce. Cholera caused many alarms, and one friend in Philadelphia died of the disease twelve hours after they had been talking together at a party. Once he was making a short journey in hill country by one of the first railways, when his carriage was derailed and he just escaped having his legs crushed. Yet he enjoyed the journey immensely, and felt the vitality and courage of the people who were achieving such an incredible conquest of the wilderness. Some of his observations are odd and quaint. Two must suffice as examples. 'Scarcely one obscene word observed throughout the States.' 'The Americans reckon to admire ladies of slender make and pale faces. Mrs Dean said she knew a young healthy blooming robust girl from England, who had recourse to large quantities of vinegar; at the same time girding herself very tight, so that she was now so reduced that she would not suppose that she could live very long.' He returned to England in the 'Hibernia'.

Robert Heywood found his stepmother seriously ill when he returned from America, and although she recovered for the moment, she died in 1836. Soon afterwards 'Sister and her son John and daughter Mary return (to Southport) leaving me truly lonely'. For the next twelve years he lived alone in the family house, his household managed by Betty the housekeeper, an old family servant. He and his sister Hannah visited each other frequently. Their route from Bolton to Southport at this time is not without interest; from Bolton to Leigh by train, thence by packet boat on the canal to Scarisbrick, four miles from Southport, where they were usually met by Hannah's coachman with the phaeton. Hannah was rather a dim woman, frequently ill. Her inheritance of £15,000 from her father (Robert had £21,000) enabled her husband John McKeand to live as a gentleman in the growing seaside village, already the favourite holiday resort of the most respectable Mancunians and Boltonians. The money remained in the business, and Robert sent Hannah £750 a year, in regular instalments paid in banknotes of £50 or £100, which were sent in halves in two separate letters.

Heywood had no other close relatives with whom he maintained an equal friendship. A good many of his nearer relatives were ne'erdowells or poor and well-meaning. He gave out magisterial admonitions to the first and modest loans or gifts to the second, always with plenty of good advice; he took his position as virtual head of the family very seriously. In 1833 his diary records: 'Settled a pension of 6d. a day on uncle James Stott.' He could be hard with the intemperate or the improvident, often refusing help altogether, and expecting his loans to be repaid; sometimes he took legal action if they were not. On one occasion in sending a gift of £20 to a Unitarian minister in difficulties he wrote a severe note. 'The Missionary Society I am told are greatly dissatisfied with the expenses incurred by you, and from my own observation I cannot but fear there is too much cause for such dissatisfaction. Why should you indulge so much or at all in the habit of smoking? It is not needed for health and besides the expense it often leads to other excesses... You must excuse me if I mention two other circumstances which I dare say you will consider very trivial but which I could not help thinking at the time indicated a thoughtless if not a most improvident disposition — the very needless and unusual expense of curling your hair and the reluctance you manifested to carry even so short a distance a few books just presented to you.'

His letters of advice might lead one to believe that Robert Heywood was a severe puritan, but this was by no means the case. The lively interest which inspired his travels led him also to attend spectacles of all kinds, race meetings at Epsom, coursing at Southport, great country houses, opera, ballet, plays and concerts. Bolton did not cater adequately for his cultural tastes, although occasionally good companies visited the local theatre. Once Charles Keen played the lead in six Shakespearian plays in one week! There were no orchestral concerts, and visiting vocal performers were often on the level of the Infant Sappho, who 'warbled her artless numbers' at the Little Bolton Town Hall on various occasions over a surprising length of time. Heywood was a keen attender at theatres and concerts. For his own satisfaction he played the organ installed at Newport Terrace. He belonged to a discussion group called the Delta Society, and he took part in Shakespearian play readings. He collected a large library of books, and every morning before breakfast did some solid reading.

In 1829 Heywood had acquired the ground for a garden on Bolton Moor, about a mile from his home, and he took a great interest in its development. He built a greenhouse and a hothouse, and laid out fishponds in the stream. His only known correspondence with William Hulton was a complaint that Hulton's workmen had discharged water containing sulphur from mine workings into the stream, and all his fish had been killed by the polluted water. He employed a good gardener James Mosley, and was soon winning prizes at the shows of the Bolton Floral and Horticultural Society. For five successive years Mosley won the award for the gardener who grew the largest number of prizewinning plants. In one year Heywood picked over a hundred bunches of grapes from his vines. He liked to have picnics in the garden, with homegrown strawberries.

Heywood was an enthusiastic fisherman. For serious fishing he usually went to his own reservoir at Entwistle. One episode shows not only his interest in fishing but his fondness for children. A boy who lived at Entwistle had been sent home from his boarding school by an outbreak of measles, and wrote to say that he would like Heywood's company for a day's fishing, as his father had given him some fly fishing tackle. His father after reading the letter added a footnote: 'Annie is in tears because James has not done what she desired, namely given her love to you. I feel disposed to whip him for his schoolboy impertinence. He seems quite unconscious of that deference which is due to either age, character or station.' Heywood replied to the boy: 'I shall have great pleasure in spending an early day with you but not as a professor in the art of fly fishing. My talents are of a lower order, what is called bottom fishing, or perhaps more correctly described as "a worm at one end and a fool at the other".... Your father's censure of the jocular part of your note was uncalled for... Present my kind regards to Pa, Ma and Sis and tell the little lady she must carry the worms.'

Of course Heywood continued to travel. He went to the British Association meetings each year; when they were held at Cork in 1843 he toured Ireland afterwards. Among many lesser expeditions were frequent visits to London, combining business and politics with pleasure. He had intended going abroad in 1840, but gave up the plan when he accepted the mayoralty. His next big expedition was a tour of the Levant with Charles Darbishire in 1845. On the way at Cadiz they went to a bull fight, but 'I rushed out, being sickened with the brutal scene'. On the steamship from Gibraltar the passengers included 'a great many foolish young sparks going to the Indies', and Lord Longford, 'a foolish mustachioed drinking simpleton', going to the Persian embassy. 'They little suppose how I look down on such self-important creatures.' They had an uncomfortable journey from Alexandria to Cairo. 'The accommodation in these boats is very indifferent, filled with vermin, cockroaches, rats etc., all upon a large scale, and the provisions so execrable that there appeared a greater chance of being eaten than of getting anything to eat.' Even at the famous Shepheard's Hotel at Cairo he had to 'brush off large cockroaches', but the landlord arranged a very pleasant visit to the Pyramids, and he enjoyed the Turkish Baths.

The high spot of their Egyptian visit was an audience, on their return to Alexandria, with Mehemet Ali, the viceroy and founder of modern Egypt. 'Through an interpreter he was informed that I was a cotton manufacturer; he immediately asked what sort and whether I used Egyptian cotton, which I of course praised, but said it was not very clean.... Perceiving that this remark was not well received I added that I believed it had improved the last year or two.'

From Alexandria they voyaged to Constantinople, but because there had recently been cases of plague in Egypt they had to spend fifteen days in quarantine in a castle on a hilltop overlooking the Black Sea. During this time they made friends with a Russian fellow traveller, Count Adlerberg, son of one of the chief ministers of the Tsar, and when they visited Constantinople he introduced them to the Grand Duke Constantine, the elder brother of the Tsar, who had renounced the Russian throne. From Constantinople they returned by sea to Trieste, and after a short stay in Venice crossed Europe by Vienna and Berlin to Hamburg.

Heywood and Darbishire were the two most famous and most confirmed bachelors in Bolton. Once, when Heywood doubled his subscription to the Dispensary his suggestion that one half was for his future wife was greeted with roars of laughter. Perhaps his close involvement with his father had delayed a normal development. He was interested in women but diffident, and hinted at a disappointment in love. One entry in his diary refers obscurely to 'the proudest two-legged thing that ever wore petticoats'.

When he finally decided to propose marriage he chose Elizabeth Shawcross of Manchester. He had known her all her life — she was 32 when he proposed — and there is a record in his diary of her being brought on a visit to the Heywoods when she was two years old. The Shawcrosses were Unitarians, related to Robert's stepmother, members of Mr. Gaskell's congregation at Cross Street, and Elizabeth's father and brothers were cotton merchants with whom he had had many financial transactions, and for whom he had the greatest respect. When he went abroad Edward Shawcross, a member of the firm of Reiss and Co., arranged introductions for him to bankers and businessmen in many countries.

It was, not surprisingly, a cool courtship, preserved in a series of odd and rather amusing letters. The first of these was one written by Robert Heywood on December 30th 1847, after a visit to the Shawcrosses, to 'My dear Elizabeth', asking 'after what occurred', for an early interview. When she did not reply for three days he became impatient and alarmed, and wrote again: 'You little know how many times I have foolishly wished that ten years of my life could have been transferred to yours (no very kind wish you will say) but we are all selfish creatures and naturally resolved to remove every obstacle that stands in the way of accomplishing an important object. And although never very anxious about personal appearances I have sometimes wished for some improvement in this way and even a little more colour if it were only to recommend the great cause of temperance.' Her frigid refusal crossed this unfortunately worded appeal; she was quite at a loss to understand what had led him to believe that she had meant more than friendship.

Robert settled down to a long siege. 'I am deeply disappointed... The proposal I must confess was received much less favourably than I had anticipated, though I had not flattered myself under all the circumstances with meeting a very gracious reception.' He thought she might be too high-minded to want to take his money, and pointed out that some years before he had told his sister that he would make ample provision, in the event of his marriage, for his two nephews and his niece. To Elizabeth's next refusal he wrote: 'Your last note, though far less encouraging than I could have wished, does not lead me to despair of ultimately convincing you that the proposed union with all its disadvantages would prove happier than most others; a result which I have arrived at from a favourable opinion of our noble selves, and also from five other similar alliances that have occurred under my observation, and which I believe in every instance proved most happy.'

After this he visited Elizabeth and persuaded her to consult her brothers, of whose support he felt sure; he could not wait for the week allowed for this, but made another plea: 'Do not I beseech you permit further diffidence to restrain you from declaring in the language of our Queen on completing an Act of Parliament, "La reine le veut." She still held out, but perhaps not quite so firmly. After another visit to Manchester he wrote: 'I am delighted to think that I perceive some diminution of the opposition so strongly and I must admit naturally manifested in the first instance and trust it will soon subside altogether. In looking round for a companion I found in one or two rather favourable instances the project seriously counteracted by considerations of a family nature. In your case I need hardly say it is quite the reverse. The long intimacy that has existed and the very high regard I have entertained for you and yours, more particularly your late respected father, have contributed largely in raising you so very high in my esteem.' Elizabeth admitted all this, but denied that she had ever encouraged him: 'Did I feel less respect for you I could more easily refuse your request, which I cannot accede to indeed. Why will you not believe me? How much I wish that the question had never been asked and that we could meet unreservedly as formerly. I am very sorry to have caused you so much trouble to no purpose. I hope you will consider this answer as conclusive.'

This was very far from Robert's intention. He persuaded Elizabeth to allow him further visits, and at last, after a successful interview on 28th January, he was able to write: 'I was much pleased to witness the favourable change that has come over you which I am persuaded will go on increasing to the end of our days.' After all her hesitations, it was in fact a very happy marriage.

They were married on 5th April 1848, and set off for a honeymoon in revolutionary Europe, a journey of three months. Robert Heywood's friends had been alarmed by the risks he proposed to run. He wrote to Dr. Bowring for advice and quoted the saying: 'You may as well be killed as frightened to death.' Bowring thought that there was no danger for a pacific man like him. 'I think an Englishman little exposed to danger in any quarter.' He pointed out that passports had been abolished by the republican government in France. The journey proceeded smoothly regardless of upheavals. They went via Paris, Geneva and Turin to Rome and Naples, and returned through Milan and Como to Switzerland, and thence down the Rhine and to Brussels and Ostend. It was his wife's first visit to the Continent.

Soon after their return Hannah McKeand died at Southport. She had been ailing for years and very ill with tuberculosis for some months. The marriage must have been a shattering blow to her hopes for her own three children. John, the eldest, had worked in Heywood's bleach works at Salford since 1841, and seems to have been a considerable source of worry to his stern uncle, who strongly criticized him for smoking and for foppery in dress. He thought that John was indulged too much by his Manchester landlady, and brought him under stricter control by having him to live at Newport Terrace and travel by train to the Salford works.

It cannot have been easy for Robert Heywood to adjust to the complete change which had taken place in his life. Some of his wife's letters are critical of his lifetime habits of economy. 'What a strange man you are! You certainly do carry your ideas of economy too far. By waiting so long for a second-class train I suppose you were too late to attend the meeting on Monday evening. I wish you would be more liberal towards yourself and also towards me as far as the house is concerned.... I do not consider it any disgrace to exhibit a little taste in the arrangement of the house — it is only what most ladies wish to do.' She felt that she had to justify the hiring of a cab on one occasion.

He appears to have heeded this criticism. In 1850 he bought a carriage for £80; it was a hallmark of status in Victorian society. The next year he acquired, for £4000, 27 acres of land near his garden on Bolton Moor, pulled down the old house on the site, and built a new house, The Pike, for £2000, a solid symmetrical house which still stands as the office of an engineering firm. By this time the Heywoods had two children, John and Mary, and another son Robert was born a few years later.

8. OLD AGE

Robert Heywood lived to be 82, and enjoyed a vigorous old age. His energies were enlivened and stimulated by his young family, and his interest in public affairs remained with him to the end. His continued concern for radical causes was shown by his work for a further reform of Parliament.

In 1849 there was a by—election in Bolton, and Sir Joshua Walmsley, a very radical reformer, was the liberal candidate. Heywood was so enthusiastic that he broke his own rule and spent several days canvassing for Walmsley, who was duly elected and remained an M.P. for Bolton until 1852. His main aim in politics was to organize a new pressure group, after the collapse of Chartism, to force the whig-liberal government to carry a further reform of Parliament. Walmsley's programme was very nearly the same as that of the Chartists, but his movement had no over-tones of class war, and secured considerable middle class support. His society, eventually known as the National Parliamentary Reform Association, demanded manhood suffrage, vote by ballot, equal electoral districts, triennial parliaments, and the abolition of property qualifications for M.P's. The early supporters of the Association all came from the South and the Midlands, and its headquarters were in London. Walmsley tried to make Bolton a main centre of activity in the North, and Heywood seconded his efforts. Walmsley stayed with him when he came to Bolton, and Heywood took the chair at his meetings. As late as 1853, after he had ceased to be an M.P. for Bolton, Walmsley brought his wife and daughter to stay at The Pike.

On the whole Lancashire reformers were not prepared to adopt a virtually Chartist programme. Heywood wrote despondently of the general apathy in Bolton in 1851 — 'a considerable apathy prevailing in this quarter, the tradespeople quite absorbed in getting money and the labouring classes fully employed at good wages with provisions so cheap, they seem to think that all is going very well.' Lancashire middle class radicals were canny and practical. Walmsley succeeded in setting up a powerful Manchester committee, with George Wilson, formerly chairman of the Anti-Corn Law League, as its chairman. In December 1851, when it held a conference for northern supporters, Cobden and Bright attended; Robert Heywood was the Bolton representative. Here the resolutions, moved by John Bright, show a toning down of aims — household suffrage, some redistribution of seats.

While one attempt after another to obtain a new reform of Parliament failed, differences between northern moderates and southern extremists divided the reformers. Heywood's connection with Walmsley ceased after 1854. The next burst of activity in Bolton coincided with George Wilson's organization of the Lancashire Reformers' Union (later the National Reform Union) in 1859. This body campaigned for a £10 occupier franchise in the counties, a ratepayer franchise in the boroughs, the ballot, shorter parliaments, and a redistribution of seats. Robert Heywood was a vice-president, but failed to win over the Bolton Reform Association even to this moderate programme. As late as 1865 he was still expressing 'surprise and regret' at the general apathy among reformers. He lived to see the Second Reform Bill carried by Disraeli and the conservatives in 1867.

Robert Heywood maintained his humane liberal outlook to the end. He never lost faith in democracy, and was even converted — possibly by marriage — to the support of women's suffrage. A year before he died he brought a resolution before the Town Council opposing capital punishment, and won for it so much support that it was lost by only 16 votes to 14. In local affairs he was no longer concerned with partisan causes; the liberals were comfortably dominant most of the time, and his differences were mainly with liberal colleagues. He won immense respect as an elder statesman, even if a somewhat crotchety one, and whenever he appeared on a public platform in his last years he could always be sure of a demonstration of public sympathy and handsome tributes from other speakers.

In 1859 Heywood attended a lecture on Samuel Crompton given by G.J. French, Crompton's biographer. Heywood had known Crompton well. He had lived for years next door to the Swedenborgian chapel in Bury Street where Crompton was the organist, and had often entertained him to tea. Now he was roused by French's enthusiasm, and in the discussion that followed the lecture they decided to inaugurate a fund to provide a memorial statue. Heywood contributed liberally and worked hard to raise the money, and in 1862 the statue (the first in Bolton), the work of J. Calder Marshall, was erected and unveiled in Nelson Square. In a characteristic speech Heywood gave the credit to French, and admitted that 'as this is Bolton in the Moors we do not know much of statuary or the fine arts'. The most startling fact about this great civic occasion was that George Crompton, Samuel's son, was brought from the workhouse to join in the celebrations.

The growth of prosperity in the town had been rapid since the hungry forties, but the drying up of cotton supplies from the United States, owing to the Civil War (1861-5), caused a serious trade crisis in 1862, and the ensuing years. Once again there was widespread misery. Heywood devoted himself to its relief; not only did he give freely to charitable funds, but he attended almost daily to supervise a food distribution centre. He was still the old-fashioned economizer, and wrote to the press strenuously objecting to 'lavish expenditure' on lighting the streets during the full moon, and on excessive street sweeping. 'With so many straitened ratepayers, and hundreds of poor wanting food, such things ought not to be.'

Bolton was slow to realise the need for public open spaces, and Heywood, with his interest in sober recreation, made it one of his chief aims in this period to arouse the town to activity. In 1854 the Earl of Bradford, the biggest landowner in Bolton, opened to the public Bradford Park in the valley of the River Tonge, but he still kept the ownership, and at a later period it was closed and privately developed. Heywood had been talking for some time of the need for municipal recreation grounds when he wrote to the *Bolton Chronicle* in 1855 offering over three acres of land near The Pike to the corporation for this purpose, on condition that the corporation itself acquired two similar plots in Great and Little Bolton. He suggested, among other things, that indoor courts, lighted by gas in winter, should be built on the ground for playing 'tennis', by which he apparently meant rackets. 'While so much is doing for the mind.... I do not want to see the body neglected.' The indifference with which the proposal was received was thought by the *Chronicle* to be due to the Crimean War and a trade depression. It hung fire until he made an unconditional offer in 1862, which the Council accepted. In 1864 he persuaded them to double the size of the Heywood Recreation Ground by buying an adjoining plot, and at the same time he repeated his offer of £500 towards a similar project in Little Bolton.

To relieve unemployment during the Lancashire cotton famine Parliament passed a Public Works Act which allowed distressed manufacturing districts to borrow money on favourable terms for schemes to provide work, and the Council decided to take advantage of this to create a new large park and to build a Town Hall in the Market Square. The latter project was not even begun until two years after the end of the Civil War, but land for the park, 48 acres between Chorley New Road and the Croal, was bought in 1864. Heywood was one of the chief advocates of this project, and his own landscape gardener, Henderson of Birkenhead, was employed to lay it out. Bolton Park (now Queen's Park) occupied a fine site just west of the town centre, which has always appealed to the imagination of planners. (Lord Leverhulme offered in 1924 to construct a high-level boulevard linking the Civic Centre with the park, but his plan was rejected; Graëme Shankland has included in the present town plan an extension of the park right into the centre.) Its opening in May 1866 was a great occasion.

The day was celebrated as a public holiday. Flags and streamers were to be seen everywhere. A ceremonial procession first set out from the Market Square for Heywood Recreation Ground. There were three bands, detachments of Volunteers, and 53 carriages, with the Earl of Bradford as the chief guest. At the recreation ground Robert Heywood signed the deed of gift and spoke to the assemblage of his 'delight in out-door exercises'. He had been sorry to see so many village greens closed and all the old games laid aside. Some 'poor creatures hardly saw the light of day'. He hoped that the recreation ground would help to impart 'health, sobriety and moral improvement.'

Returning to the Square, the procession set out for Bolton Park, and was now joined by 3000 Sunday school scholars with banners. One of blue silk actually bore the device 'Excelsior', another 'Obey Your Parents'. Behind them were the Juvenile Foresters, led by four boys on ponies and two on foot dressed as Robin Hood's band, and last came the Self-actor Minders from the spinning mills. A crowd of 20,000 attended the opening ceremony at the park, performed by the Earl with a silver key. They sang the Old Hundredth, the Members of Parliament spoke, and then Heywood was called for. 'After some reluctance he gave way to the universal cheering which greeted his name', and made a brief speech. This occasion was a handsome recognition of his public-spirited career. At the ceremonial dinner Councillor Barlow, chairman of the Parks Committee, 'attributed that day's result to the persistent advocacy of recreation grounds by Alderman Heywood'.

Ever careful about expense, Heywood thought that the cost of Bolton Park, nearly £50,000, was excessive, and in particular he criticized the provision of railings and gatehouses. But if the park had to be fenced in and locked, he objected most to its being closed on Sunday morning, and in 1867 conducted a vigorous campaign for Sunday opening. In the course of this one of his supporters took a census and found that 10,000 persons entered the park on one particular Sunday afternoon. The Sunday schools in those days had both morning and afternoon sessions — at which they still taught reading and writing — and there was much opposition to a plan which might encourage truancy. The Parks Committee, to Heywood's disgust, voted by seven to three against Sunday morning opening.

The splendid Town Hall which gives distinction to the civic centre of Bolton was begun in 1867. Heywood was appalled at the proposed cost of £140,000. He thought that £50,000 would be quite enough to spend on the building, and consequently opposed the creation of the finest monument to Victorian civic pride in the town. His argument that there were many more necessary tasks to be done for the health and welfare of the public is one that it is always difficult to answer.

In his last years as earlier Robert Heywood was always ready to help in forwarding such tasks. We have already noted his strenuous activity during the cotton famine in helping to organize a food distribution centre which spent over £30,000 on relief in three years. In 1864 he gave a contribution to a new Working Men's Club, a temperance institution; at the opening he said that he would have liked to prohibit smoking, but recognized that that was impracticable — he hoped that the club would draw men away from the public house. At about the same time he gave £500 for a new building in Mawdsley Street for the Mechanics' Institute, on condition that they arranged classes for women, and this was agreed to by the committee. (The building was later used as Bolton's first Technical College.) In the last year of his life he assisted in the founding of the Institute for the Blind, and his wife became a member of the committee. He also became a trustee for Dr. Chadwick's model working class dwellings, which were being built near his home. At this time he was planning to set up at his own expense the public wash-houses which he had advocated unsuccessfully for so long. His last benefaction, within a week of his death, was a gift of £1000 to the Infirmary when he offered his resignation from the office of secretary which he had held for 55 years; the committee would not allow him to resign, and he died in office. Appropriately a ward in the present Royal Infirmary is named after him.

Amid all his more public interests, Robert Heywood never neglected Bank Street Chapel. The annual Sunday school treat was held at Whitsuntide at The Pike at his expense. He gave a large proportion of the money needed for rebuilding the chapel in 1851, and in 1866 he bought a public house next door — the chapel was originally hemmed in by public houses — to provide a site for a new Sunday school.

After Robert Heywood's marriage business affairs took up very little of his time. Since Charles Darbishire's resignation of his partnership in John Heywood and Son, Heywood had employed a manager. In 1854, when machine production had at last made it obsolete, he closed down this manufacturing business. His other big interest was the Crescent Bleachworks in Salford, acquired in 1839 when James Slater went bankrupt. He employed a first-rate manager, William Mosley, and the bleaching business weathered the slump and became profitable; it never occupied much of his time. (His youngest son Robert eventually bought the business from the other heirs and managed it for many years.) His fortune accumulated to over £100,000 at the time of his death. No doubt, although after his marriage he lived in a much grander style, he was still very careful about expense.

One form of expense which he never denied himself was travel. Apart from innumerable visits to London, he still went to the British Association meetings every year and continued to plan enterprising holidays, and kept up this active life into his eighties. In 1855 he visited Paris with Charles Darbishire, and he was there again in 1860. In 1857 he had a holiday in Killarney after the British Association meetings in Dublin, and he made the famous excursion through the Gap of Dunloe on foot. In 1858 he took his wife to Russia, a country not much visited by Englishmen in those days just after the Crimean War. They failed to meet his former acquaintance Count Adlerberg, who was away from St. Petersburg attending the Tsar on a journey. From St. Petersburg they paid a visit to Moscow. Later holidays more frequently included the children — Scotland, the Lake District, North Wales and the Isle of Man — they were strenuous walking holidays in hill country. He climbed Snowdon at the age of 76 without the help of a stick; he and the children got to the top in 3½ hours and came down in two. In the last months of his life he visited London for a conference in May 1868, was in North Wales in June, in Herefordshire and Monmouthshire in July, and at the British Association meeting at Norwich in September. At the age of 82 he displayed an almost Gladstonian vigour.

Robert Heywood was taken ill less than a month before his death. During this illness he said: 'My life has been one long summer day, but I do not wish it further prolonged.' He died on 26th October 1868. The funeral was an occasion for a public demonstration of the respect in which he was held in Bolton. Nearly all the leading men of the town were there: 35 carriages followed the hearse. Shops in the town centre were shut for two hours, and crowds lined the route of the funeral procession. The local newspapers appeared with black edging.

Among the many fine tributes paid to Robert Heywood at the time of his death, two appear to sum up the things for which he is worth remembering. The *Bolton Evening News* said: 'Few men have deserved better of their own generation than the venerable man whose rising in any assembly of his fellow-townsmen was the signal for those demonstrations of friendly feeling and goodwill which are solely awarded to those who have won the hearts of the community. He was one of a thousand. As a genial, pleasant-spoken, interesting companion he had few superiors.

He had read books and men to good purpose. His mind had been enlarged by travel in many lands... He possessed a large share of that racy humour and sharp wit which is one of the prevailing characteristics of the true Lancashireman.' The *Bolton Chronicle* wrote his epitaph: 'He was an active promoter of every institution for the intellectual and moral improvement of the people of his native town. To give a detailed biography of such a life would be to write the local history of our time.'

INDEX